Work in Progress

work in progress

The Road to Empowerment, The Journey Through Shame

Dr. Abbie Maroño

NEW YORK

LONDON • NASHVILLE • MELBOURNE • VANCOUVER

Work in Progress

The Road to Empowerment, The Journey Through Shame

Published in New York, New York, by Morgan James Publishing. Morgan James is a trademark of Morgan James, LLC. www.MorganJamesPublishing.com

Proudly distributed by Publishers Group West®

Morgan James BOGO™

A **FREE** ebook edition is available for you or a friend with the purchase of this print book.

CLEARLY SIGN YOUR NAME ABOVE

Instructions to claim your free ebook edition:
1. Visit MorganJamesBOGO.com
2. Sign your name CLEARLY in the space above
3. Complete the form and submit a photo of this entire page
4. You or your friend can download the ebook to your preferred device

ISBN 9781636983325 paperback
ISBN 9781636983332 ebook
Library of Congress Control Number: 2023946752

Cover & Interior Design by:
Christopher Kirk
www.GFSstudio.com

Editors:
Corrine Hickin and
Raymond Pendleton

Morgan James PUBLISHING Builds with... **Habitat for Humanity®** Peninsula and Greater Williamsburg

Morgan James is a proud partner of Habitat for Humanity Peninsula and Greater Williamsburg. Partners in building since 2006.

Get involved today! Visit: www.morgan-james-publishing.com/giving-back

I dedicate this book, and every book that follows, to my dear father. There is nothing more and nothing less to say than this; You and I against the world.

To my amazing team of editors, I couldn't have done it without you. Thank you.
Corrine Hickin
Virginia Combs
Andy Earle
Ray Pendleton

Table of Contents

Acknowledgments

To my father; there are some families that forget to tell each other how much they mean to one another because they think there will always be more time. We are not one of those families. Since I left for university, 8 years ago, not a day has passed where we don't communicate our love and appreciation for one another. I couldn't imagine my mornings without a call or text from you with our obligatory "love and miss you" or our routine check ins to make sure the other is safe as the sun goes down. I know that I can count on you when I need you, whether it's for a word of reassurance, a rant about my day, a cat sitter, a shoulder to cry on, or a hand moving 5000 miles across the globe, you are by my side without hesitation. So much of what I have achieved has been to make you proud, and in the process, I have learned to be proud of myself. Thank you for continuing to fight through the times you felt broken and plagued by thoughts of giving up, I know it was me (and my sisters) you were fighting for, not yourself.

I couldn't imagine a love stronger than the love we share. Thank you.

To my beautiful sisters; it doesn't matter how much space there is between us, or how many oceans we are apart, our love remains strong. Through thick and thin. I love you both.

It is rare to find people who truly want to support you and watch you shine. I have been lucky enough to find that in you, Joe and Thryth Navarro. Joe, you truly are one of a kind; you inspire me every day with your intellect, curiosity, and dedication to your craft. Thryth, you embody everything that I hope to one day be; you are strong, kind, intelligent, and loving. You are an inspiration in so many ways, yet you do not see how powerful you are. Thank you for showing me that it really *is* possible to do it all.

To Chris Hadnagy, I could so easily write paragraphs on how thankful I am to you for bringing me into a company I love, providing me career opportunities, and putting up with my aggressive love for science, but whilst all of that is true, none of it compares to how grateful I am for your friendship. You provided me with a safe space to grow, you never judged, only listened and supported. I am sorry that the past couple of years have not shown you the kindness you deserve, but I hope the world opens their eyes to your true, kind nature.

To David Keatley, I've said it before and I will say it again, I could thank you on every piece of work I produce and it would still never be enough. Whenever I look back on the growth of my career, you've always been there propelling me forward and cheering me on. The best choice I ever made was coming to you after that lecture with the idea that started it all. Without your support, I would not be where I am today. You inspired me then and you inspire me now.

Robin Dreeke, I am not sure I have ever met anyone who gets as excited about the field of trust as much as you and I. Thank you for the kindness you showed me, and for inspiring me with a continued source of love and passion for your craft.

Jordyn, there is no other woman like you. Our friendship is truly special, and I would wholeheartedly trust you with my life. Thank you for being the best friend anyone could ever ask for. I do not deserve you, but I hope that one day I do.

Finally, thank you to the person reading this now. Thank you for believing in my work enough to read this book. I hope that my words bring you understanding, comfort, and healing. I hope that as you finish this book, you finish it a kinder, more empowered person.

Introduction

*"Owning our story and loving ourselves through that
process is the bravest thing that we will ever do."*
–Brene Brown, *The Gifts of Imperfection*

When humans meet a new person, it takes 33 milliseconds for us to decide if we trust them. Before a full second passes, our brains decide whether they consider this stranger a threat, a nuisance, or a cooperator. We do this unconsciously by picking up small nonverbal cues—a genuine smile, an open posture, or even a small gesture of comfort like offering a cup of coffee—that are considered signals of trustworthiness.

Trust is a key factor in communication. When you trust someone, you feel safe with them. At the root of the human experience is the need to feel safe. Humans' survival instincts rely on trusting people to raise the odds of survival.

The way we trust ourselves is more complicated. Our sense of trust doesn't manifest in the first 33 milliseconds we're alive.

1

For the first few years of any person's existence, we don't have a conscious understanding of trust or trustworthiness. In fact, most of the interactions we have with ourselves aren't indicators usually considered trustworthy.

In my life, I spend most of my "me time" criticizing myself. Would I allow someone I trusted to treat me this way? Of course not. But I make special permissions for myself, for reasons that can only be explained (in a way I'll accept) through science. When I look in the mirror, I don't meet my own gaze with a smile. Most of the time, my brow furrows and I lean in close—which, if anyone else did, would seem threatening. *Is that a pimple? Am I getting frown lines? Wow, I need a haircut.* Inside, my brain sees me pick myself apart. I don't even realize it on a conscious level, but I pit my brain against myself and appear less trustworthy…to me.

Trust builds over time as we see consistency. This is true for the trust we place in others and in ourselves. People who are consistently loyal, kind, and compassionate demonstrate their trustworthiness and build strong social bonds. When they stray from those behaviors, their trustworthiness decreases. The same is true about our own behaviors—and that's where shame comes into play.

The tricky part of trust is that no one is consistent all the time. You may not notice it in your parents, your best friends, or your partner, but you spend all of your time with yourself. You know your own moments of inconsistency better than anyone else's. This knowledge makes it hard to build trust in yourself, and it makes it easier to feel ashamed of those moments of inconsistency.

Shame is the emotional result of behaviors that are inconsistent with who we want to be. The version of ourselves we long to trust makes us feel safe, comfortable, and confident. When we act against this version, shame is the brain's attempt to nudge us back in the right direction. Shame is a human condition, and we could all stand to learn more about it. Even I learn more about shame's relationship to empowerment, resiliency, and trust every day, and I'm a bona fide expert.

Trusting yourself takes years, and sometimes, shame can make it harder to trust yourself than to trust other people. There is a whole market out there full of celebrities, influencers, and self-proclaimed "experts" who want you to trust them, but aren't concerned with whether you trust yourself. They teach empowerment without helping their audience learn how to overcome a lack of self-trust and an abundance of shame. By ignoring the very thing stopping you from reaching empowerment, they also stop you from learning you are someone worthy of your own trust.

Our brains don't put energy into making us feel any emotion just for us to ignore it. Shame is not a barrier on the journey to empowerment; it's a mandatory stop along the way. Shame is not an emotion we can ignore, avoid, or outright dismiss if we want to achieve lasting change. The best way to move through shame and reach empowerment is to understand why we feel shame, why it's normal, and how to deal with it in a healthy way.

I'm always disappointed in books that try to help the audience discover themselves by offering empty promises and ignoring the science behind why it's such a difficult undertaking in the first place. These books offer motivation, but they wave a hand over the more painful parts of self-discovery—like shame. They create fragile empowerment that only holds strong as long as nothing in life ever goes wrong again. It's not realistic.

Many of the other books about empowerment sell the concept like they're selling bottled water from the Fountain of Youth. It's elusive, exciting, and only attainable if you buy now! The promise of empowerment is alluring—no one sees the potential for confidence, autonomy, and self-assurance and says, "no thanks, I like hating myself just fine!"

Unsurprisingly, there is a growing interest in the pursuit of empowerment. The concept is popular among many academics and practitioners who are keen to uncover the secrets of living unapologetically. It's more common to hear about empowerment on podcasts, TV shows, and mindfulness meditation retreats. But how much of it is the real deal, and how much of it can we find flowing out of our own faucets at home?

As a scientist, I deal with what can be explored, studied, and proven. I love references. I love cold, hard facts. I love the tangible and the true. I became a Professor of Psychology at twenty-three years old and obtained a PhD in Psychology shortly after. I've lived and breathed psychology with nothing but passion and excitement since then, and it has helped create the self-concept I love and trust today.

I became a university lecturer (in America you call them professors) by the time I was twenty-three. That same year, I owned my first house. I earned my doctorate. I published several academic papers before my twentieth birthday. I worked with the world's leading experts in my field, who came to me for answers to their scientific questions.

I'm not telling you this to brag, I promise. Although I accomplished more than my younger self could have ever imagined, never once did I stop to celebrate any of it. Every accomplishment was overshadowed by whatever goal I set next for myself. The more people appreciated me, the more people praised me, the worse I felt. I felt like a fraud, hiding my mistakes behind my back and hoping no one would walk around me. It took a long time for me to realize why I felt I couldn't stop pushing myself—if I turned to look back, I might see parts of my shameful past. I could turn to reminisce about Lecturer Abbie, but I might also catch a glimpse of Party Girl Abbie, Drug Addict Abbie, or College Dropout Abbie. And those weren't girls I wanted to see again.

I thought if I kept working, kept running from my past, I could stack up the good deeds to bury the bad. I stopped my career progression because I didn't want to sit in front of a camera while the full force of people's opinions came down on me. I didn't form relationships with anyone because I was afraid one look too long would reveal all the darkness, shame, and regret inside of me. I didn't want to be found out. But I eventually realized I needed to stop, unpack, and let the light in, before someone else did it for me.

That's why I want to be the one to tell my story. This is my narrative and it's time for me to take control, just as it's time for you to take control of yours. I was tired of living a life of shame, guilt, and isolation, and I don't want anyone else to feel they need to live that way, either. We all make mistakes. We're all imperfect. We're all working to be the best version of ourselves, but we cannot let our past and our shame stop us from making progress. We can take this journey together and come out the other side feeling empowered.

Every concept covered in this book is backed by scientific data and years of clinical research. Some of these studies I've conducted myself. And as a woman navigating the world of science and business, I'll also cover my experiences therein. I cried as I wrote many of these pages, and I laughed as I wrote others. I hope my journey will help you while you take a journey of your own.

Reaching empowerment is tough. Processing shame is tougher. The journey is messy. Sometimes, it feels impossible. But it's necessary, and it's worth doing the right way. If we take shortcuts, if we ignore the problem to snatch up the solution, we're doomed to restart the process as soon as we act out of character and feel shame again.

Taking the journey toward empowerment would be impossible without a map to guide you. You can't travel in one direction and blindly hope you'll make it somewhere safe. By understanding your emotional experience, your inner mechanisms and drivers, and your own self-concept, you build a map to guide you toward a life of unapologetic, confident living.

Once you know what we're dealing with inside yourself, you can use the information to build up some resilience. I won't lie to you—this takes time and dedication. Pain is there, difficult feelings are there, but they don't have to control you; you can control them. As you travel toward the version of yourself that brings comfort and joy, you will also learn to work through the hurtful words and actions of others. You'll look at why you care what others think and say about you, and, perhaps contradictorily, why it isn't in your nature to ignore those judgments.

I want you to understand why you care about the words of others, why some people are kind and others are cruel, and how to see shame and deal with it in a healthy way. You can show love and kindness without allowing people to take advantage if you know your boundaries. You can embrace empowerment as a form of self-reflection, self-acceptance, kindness, and resilience.

This might all sound rather daunting, but you won't be traveling this road alone. I'll be beside you. The journey is not a short one, but the knowledge you collect along the way will help you through the dark passages of your own past.

To reach true empowerment, you must face the older versions of you who made you feel shame. You'll have to confront your own personas, whether they're Drug Dealer Dave, Alcoholic Aly, Big Bully Beth, or some equally shameful iteration of your growth process. Harder still, you're not confronting these alter egos with admonition—you're embracing them, showing them kindness, and making peace with their place among the rest of your selves. Doing this is the only way through. I would know—I went from Piggy in the Middle Abbie to Doctor Abbie, and I'm going to show you how.

I could make all sorts of claims about what changes you'll be able to make if you read my book (and I will!), but for you to believe, it's important for me to be honest about myself, where I came from, and the struggles I've faced along the way. In these next ten chapters, I'm going to be more open with you than I've ever been with anyone. There are some people out there who have known me my whole life, and they're going to learn some things about me they've never heard before.

No matter what you've been through, no matter what you've achieved (or haven't), where you are, or who you've been—you can be a better, kinder, happier version of yourself. The first step is to accept that you're never finished growing. You're always a work in progress—just like everyone else.

Chapter 1

Defining Shame, Resilience, and Empowerment

"If you believe that feeling bad or worrying long enough will change a past or future event, you are residing on another planet with a different reality system."
—William James

I don't like looking back to my childhood. My early years were lonely and empty. Even now, when I try to conjure specific memories from the first decade of my life, I can't recall details. My childhood memories return to me as blurry shapes lost in a thick fog, like gnarled trees in a hazy forest.

My sharpest memories are full of shouting. My parents were angry a lot back then. My dad was an intense man, and he both loved and raged with fierceness. He would well up when he thought about the love he had for his kids, but he was also quick to rip phones off the wall when agents put him on hold, or punch holes in walls and doors during arguments with my mum. His tirades were terrifying, but I was not afraid of him hurting us. My dad never once raised a hand in anger to me, my sister, or my mom. He was angry, not violent.

My mother was angry too, but hers was a quiet, biting anger. Unlike my dad, my mum's anger was often directed at her children. She had no trouble screaming at us, swearing at us, insulting us, or reminding us how little she cared. Over the years, her rage crystallized into bitterness and spite. And when she drank, which was often, her anger put my dad's to shame.

My parents split up when I was still very young. Dad struggled with the separation and moved from the UK to America. When I try to think back and remember my age when he left, my age when he returned, and my age when I first recognized my depression, I can't put a number to any of it.

I developed some attachment issues as a result of my unstable home life. I couldn't bring my parents to infant school with me, so instead, I carried around cuddly toys everywhere I went. I had a whole bag of stuffed animals I never let leave my sight. At the time I didn't put much thought into my obsession with them, but looking back now, it's clear my cuddly toys were my safety. They gave me a sense of consistency my parents did not. My toys never took it in turn to shout at me and leave. I trusted them.

Although my toys brought me comfort, they also brought unwanted attention. Kids would take my toys from me and throw them out of my reach, laughing at my panicked cries to give them back. One of their favorite games was "piggy in the middle," where they played catch with my toys over my head to keep them from me. I'd tell myself we were all playing together, but deep down I knew I wasn't playing—I was the one being played with.

Somewhere along the fuzzy timeline of my childhood, Dad returned from America. I think he wanted to put the family back together. Unfortunately for him, in a true, sitcom fashion, Mum was busy having an affair with the window cleaner. When Dad came back, he took custody of me and my sisters. We didn't have a lot of money from that point, and Dad struggled with his health, but he never asked for child support from my mother. He didn't want anything from her; he just wanted his girls.

Comprehensive school (that's what us Brits call high school) came around for me, and I still kept my cuddly toys with me. I didn't keep them in my arms—I learned to tuck them away in my backpack. I still had them for support, but as long as no one else saw them, I could keep my shameful stuffies to myself.

Hiding my toys didn't make me invisible, though. I was still an odd kid. I was an easy target for bullies. I was quiet, shy, and self-conscious. I was what some people call a "late bloomer," which meant my body stayed childish while my classmates developed curvy hips and chests. My clothes were all hand-me-downs from my older sisters, who were not late bloomers. Everything I wore bulged and stretched in the wrong places. I felt like an outsider, and the other kids read my insecurities as if they were printed on my forehead.

The bullies at school served mixed insults to me. I was shamed for being small some days, and other days I was called fat. Some said I must be anorexic while others laughed across the cafeteria at the nerdy girl eating lunch alone.

"What a pig!" they laughed, and suddenly I was the piggy in the middle again, sitting helplessly while they lobbed insults back and forth above me. They wanted me to react. They wanted to get a rise out of the girl with the books and the bag full of toys. I stayed quiet, hoping I could somehow disappear into my backpack, too.

I didn't catch a break from the bullies until my body began changing. Once the change started, I developed quickly. Instantly, boys paid attention to me—girls, too. One girl, I'll call her Melanie, was the first to change her tune. She had always been especially nasty to me, but the moment I moved up from a training bra, she started sitting with me at lunch.

Melanie was pretty enough, but her real power came from how she talked to our classmates. She was bubbly to the right people and cruel to the ones she thought were below her. She radiated confidence in a way that both baffled me and made me jealous. I'd watch her joke around with the other girls in class and think, *how is she doing that? Why can't I do that?* I couldn't hold a single conversation without stuttering or trailing off before I finished talking. I could only handle short exchanges before I felt the urge to disappear. But Melanie had it all figured out. In fact, the more I paid attention, the more it seemed like *everyone* had it figured out.

Everyone but me.

I felt alone. I felt a deep shame about my inability to make friends or fit in at school. I didn't think there was a single person in the world who understood me. Not Melanie, not my sisters, not even my dad. When I saw myself reflected back in the eyes of other people, I didn't recognize the person I saw. *Are they wrong about me, or am I wrong about me?* My misery grew too heavy to carry. I stopped wanting to carry on at all.

Everyone feels shame. It's part of being human. It's not a comfortable feeling, but the human experience couldn't exist without it. This is a difficult concept to grasp as most people, myself included, instinctively go to great lengths to avoid feeling shame. Unfortunately, the consequences of this avoidance are crushing.

I find that while most people don't want to feel shame, few people know what they would rather feel instead. The absence of a feeling is numbness, and I don't know many people who would admit wanting to feel numb. I think there is a word for the feeling we shame-fleers want, though—it's been popping up in science and popular culture more frequently in recent years: empowerment.

Empowerment is a big word that's thrown around in a variety of contexts. But what does it mean? And how does it relate to shame? These are two questions I've pondered and studied at great lengths. What I've found is that you can't reach empowerment by ignoring shame.

Shame feels like an emotion to avoid—it's discomfort, it's self-reflection, it's a form of humility. When shame makes our cheeks flush and twists up our stomachs, the last thing we want to do is face it, or talk about it with others. We pack it away in the corners of our minds, and we try not to look at it. However, the more we hide our shame, the bigger the shame grows.

It's no surprise humans aren't keen to share their shame with others. We're taught that we can ignore shame and lead a happy life without it. When influencers, celebrities, and self-proclaimed experts on the human experience talk about empowerment, they leave shame out of the conversation. Shame is the elephant in the room, the opposite of empowerment. How can you be empowered if you're worried about how you look, what kind of car you drive, or how much money you make? How can you be empowered if you care what other people think?

Most guides to empowerment are filled with shame-shunning practices. *You have to ignore your self-doubt! Fight back against your inner voice! Wring out your Shame Sham-Wow!* These lessons teach people to turn their backs on shame and never look at it again. That's not real growth, and it's certainly not real empowerment. All it takes to break down that kind of empowerment is a swift shame-kick in the pants.

There's a reason these guides' advice feels flimsy: they ignore the science behind *why* people feel shame. They pretend shame is avoidable. They tell you to put on your running shoes and run from your shame. If it can't catch you, it doesn't exist, right?

But while you're running from your shame, your shame is growing. That pile of shameful memories becomes a mountain, and the longer you hide from it, the sooner you'll have nowhere left to run. When it finally catches up to you, it's going to crush you.

When "experts" claim they live a shame-free life, what they're actually saying is they're avoiding a crucial part of their emotional experience. They pretend emotions are controllable at all times. In reality, you have no control over why you feel the way you feel. The systems in charge of emotional responses are so complex, even the most emotionally aware person on the planet isn't fully conscious of what happens in their brain before it responds. Emotions are not designed to be ignored, and ignoring them does not build any control over them. The control comes *after* the emotional response, and only once the response is fully understood.

The only way to remedy your emotions is to understand them: why you feel them, how they help you, and how to move past them. You must understand the mechanisms that create your emotional responses. It's one thing to tell yourself you don't feel worthy of an emotion, or that you don't understand why you feel a specific emotion, but the emotion is happening for a reason. It's not going anywhere until you figure it out.

Take anger for example: you might get angry at a small inconvenience, like a stubborn jar lid or a key that won't turn. You're mad you can't get the thing to work, but you know it's not worth being mad about, so you get mad at yourself, too. Now you're thinking about all the other times you've cursed at jars and keys and twist ties and USB plugs that won't go in no matter which way you flip them. You're mad at yourself for being mad about being mad. It makes you feel like something is broken inside.

Anger is an emotional response designed to protect you; it has a purpose. The pickle jar might not be trying to attack you, but the anger you feel is your mind saying, "Hey, let's take a break before you hurt yourself." Once you comprehend that, you can step outside the anger cycle. You know you're not broken; you're not malfunctioning. You're simply responding.

In today's society, people are only willing to share their positive emotional responses with others. It's easy for your feelings to seem out of place when your social media is cluttered with people living their best lives. People aren't sharing photos of their snotty noses and tear-streaked eyes on Instagram. No one posts their fitness journey until they're far enough along to see noticeable progress. No one is broadcasting their *true* shame for all to see. If they *do* share a shameful story, it's one with a happy ending.

"I learned a valuable lesson, and now I'm even better than before!"

Meanwhile, you're sitting on your couch with a rock in your gut, scrolling as fast as possible to the next post before you have to think about your own shame.

What is wrong with me?

There is nothing wrong with you. Your shame, your guilt, your discomfort with negative feelings are all evolutionary tools humans need to survive and thrive. The complex systems ruling over our emotions and states of mind are products of generations of evolution. What we experience today has been tried and tested for thousands of years, and the systems still exist because they have served humanity to keep us alive, engaged, and evolving.

Recognizing your emotional responses, acknowledging their purpose, and addressing them directly is a form of resilience. Resilience is a crucial part of being truly empowered. Resilience doesn't function the way other guides to empowerment make it seem—it isn't about being bulletproof to the thoughts, feelings, or words of others. It's not about deflecting shameful thoughts or ignoring negative emotions. True resilience doesn't stop you from getting knocked down. True resilience helps you get back up.

Shame and Resilience

Shame is one of the more uncomfortable emotions a human can experience. There are competing definitions for shame in academic literature, but in general, shame is considered a self-conscious emotion involving a negative evaluation of one's behavior or oneself, usually arising from a moral or social transgression.

That definition is clinical and impersonal, and it makes shame sound less vivid and painful than what most people experience. I prefer Brene Brown's definition of shame: "the intensely painful feeling or experience of believing we are flawed and therefore unworthy of love and belonging."

Every time you feel shame, you're faced with a choice: you can hide from it, or you can face it. Hiding from shame feels like the easier option—no need to examine whether you're *actually* unworthy of love or belonging based on your actions. No need to make tough changes to the way you think, act, or feel. However, hiding from your shame stops you from growing. It hinders your relationships with other people. It may relieve short-term discomfort, but you're only delaying an inevitable breakdown.

Shame lets you know your actions are causing harm, whether it's to yourself or to others. When you choose to face your shame, you begin a reflective process that helps you minimize harm and better understand yourself. If you self-reflect and realize your actions are aligned with your sense of who you are, and you're not causing any intentional harm to anyone, you can stand strong in your beliefs and behaviors. If your actions do not align with your sense of self, you can make a change for the better.

If you don't consider the effects of your behavior on yourself and other people, your ability to have successful relationships will suffer. Think about the people you know who seem totally unaware of how they affect others. They're usually self-absorbed, inconsiderate, or downright rude. They're not at the top of anyone's list for friends or partners. If you're not willing to reflect on your own actions, you're not far off from them. Your place in your community will disappear, and your fears of isolation and unworthiness will become a reality. Self-reflection is a big part of how humans survive together.

Facing shame feels scary, but it's a necessary function of social society. If people didn't feel shame, our society would crumble. No one would think twice about lying, stealing, cheating, or hurting others. There would be no sense of trust between friends, family, or even strangers. Our saving grace as a society is that most people like to feel good about themselves. If no one reflected on whether their actions made them feel like a good person, we wouldn't have good people, plain and simple.

So, how can you face your shame and grow as a person? By being resilient.

Resilience is more than recovering from adversity or bouncing back after failure. It is a state of mind that promotes a willingness to grow. When shame feels sharp and painful, resilience acts as a suit of armor. It's not impenetrable, but it is a tool that protects you on your reflective journey.

Being resilient is a choice, but it's not a choice you make once: you choose resilience each time you feel your emotions taking over. You choose resilience when you stop fighting the pickle jar and ask for help. You choose resilience when you apologize for hurting someone else, even if it wasn't intentional. You choose resilience when you can accept your actions as wrong without letting them change your self-perception.

Resilience does not make you bulletproof; it does not protect you from feeling shame. Instead, resilience helps you recover from the painful sting of shame by reminding you that what you *did* is not who you *are*. Resilience is knowing your own worth, knowing your own value, and being able to honestly recognize your own efforts to be the best version of yourself. When you can look at yourself in the mirror and recognize that the person looking back at you is trying to be better, you are practicing resilience.

Outside the realm of psychology, resilience carries a similar meaning. Resilient code in programming refers to techniques that enable software applications or systems to withstand errors, failures, or adverse conditions with minimal disruptions. These systems are designed to mitigate risk, improve conditions, and redirect around obstacles. When code is resilient, it is flexible enough to encounter issues and move through them to return desired results.

Self-resilience is not dissimilar from resilient code. When your thoughts, feelings, and actions interact with each other, sometimes you achieve a positive result, and sometimes you receive a negative one. Practicing resilience helps you figure out which parts of your system are missing, malfunctioning, or overpowering other parts. Once you pinpoint the point of failure, you can adapt to avoid it. This process doesn't make any fundamental changes to who you are, but it does allow you to function better. And the better you function in the face of failure, the closer you are to achieving empowerment.

There's a cliché I hear often, and every time I hear it, it sounds like nails on a chalkboard.

"Take me as I am or not at all."

At first listen, that proclamation *sounds* like empowerment. It seems like the person is so confident in who they are, they feel no need to make adjustments to make others happy. They are claiming to be a finished person, and they're not interested in hearing otherwise. No work in progress here—they're all done.

While it might sound nice at first, the true message is one of selfishness and lacks any self-awareness. What right does anyone have to force others to grow around them? Why would anyone accept a relationship with a person who announces they're unwilling to adapt to their interests, comforts, or needs? If you think you're immune to the human conditions of bias, imperfection, or humility, you're well on your way to psychopathy.

If you go down the dangerous path of believing the whole world exists to validate you while you can't be bothered to work on yourself, you'll never reach empowerment. It's ironic: if you fall for the cliches that say you don't need to change, you're probably one of the people who need to change the most.

So, what is empowerment, if not a shameless declaration of self-adoration? The answer is elusive. Academics at the University of Connecticut compiled all of the known research studies on empowerment in the hope of uncovering a definition.[1] To their dismay, they still didn't get a clear answer. It turns out there is no clear, universally agreed-upon definition of the concept of empowerment.

The lack of definition challenges scholars, so they avoided nailing down a definition at all. It's almost as if they're saying, *it can't be defined, so let's not try. Let's just use a partial, inconclusive, constricted interpretation and hope for the best.* That might work as clickbait; it might draw in people who desperately want to access this elusive empowerment elixir, but it's lazy and inaccurate. How can anyone be empowered if they don't know what empowerment means?

Some people believe empowerment is the sense of not caring what people think—that it means "I'm going to be shamelessly myself." Others think it means being successful, being at the top of their game, or having financial stability. Some think empowerment is wrapped up in material possessions—the most empowered people only drive Lexuses and only wear Rolexes (those people are big on "X" brands.) Other people believe the only way to be empowered is to ignore material goods completely. They believe empowerment focuses on the here and now, what you are, not what you own.

In order to work out what empowerment is, we have to first consider what it is not. The most popular definitions for empowerment focus on being static as an individual. They think empowerment means not caring what others think of you, not caring if they talk about you, gossip, or criticize, because you are you and have no intention of changing for anyone. You feel no shame for your behavior and you have the right to do what you want, when you want.

I disagree.

This individualized idea of empowerment goes against who we are as human beings. We are hard-wired to care what other people think of us. It is psychologically and neurologically rewarding to be cooperative and kind.

Maybe it's worth considering that there *is* no one definition for empowerment. Scientists, myself included, spend their whole careers defining elusive concepts. But there are cases where scientists agree to disagree on the specifics—it's why our fingers aren't numbered one through five. (Or four—does the thumb count? If it does, is that finger one or finger five? And don't get me started on the toes!)

Empowerment is a difficult concept to define because it doesn't look or feel the same for everybody. For some it's loud and for some it's quiet. It's okay for empowerment to feel different for every person—we are all unique systems, and we've all experienced different issues we've had to adapt through. Empowerment is still difficult for me to define for myself. I'm still learning how to embrace who I am every day. But I know who I am not, I know who I want to be, and I know I am on my way there.

By the end of this book, you will discover new and different answers for what empowerment means to you. You'll also have a better understanding of the relationship between shame and empowerment. You'll have the science and evidence to back up how the brain works and how your emotional experience informs who you are. These three main points will be key for your journey through shame to empowerment:

1. The empirical evidence behind why conflating empowerment with selfishness is wrong and how doing so can be harmful.
2. The ways in which shame is actually good for us and why we tend to ignore it, then react when it hurts us.
3. The recognition that our empowerment is entirely distinct from other people's; it has nothing to do with how people feel about us, how they react to us, or their opinion of us.

No matter what stage of life we're in, we're always growing. Part of growing is learning from our mistakes. That's how the world has flourished. Imagine if, after discovering the atom, we stopped digging deeper? If we'd been too scared to find something smaller at the risk of making a mistake? When we keep asking questions, keep digging a little deeper, the world changes. We change.

If you are determined to be the same as you've always been and never adapt, you will never grow. People will change around you, the world will move on and develop, but you? All you'll ever be is a missed opportunity—an outdated system without resilience or function.

Reaching Empowerment

If you're going to move forward, facing your shame with strength and the knowledge of who you are, you must first learn to deal with criticism without feeling ashamed. There will always be people who want to tear you down, there will always be people that do not want to see others succeed. You will be met with jealousy as well as personality clashes, you will be met with people who just want to throw negativity at you—but being empowered will allow you work through these difficult periods, deal with shame, recognize who you are, and help you grow.

Empowerment is not the final destination on your journey—it's a new tool to help you live your life. When you reach empowerment, you aren't finished working on yourself. No one is finished; no one reaches perfection. It's part of being a human. Empowerment helps people choose *when* to change and *how* to change. It stops others from influencing how you adapt. It keeps you flexible without jeopardizing your safety or comfort. Empowerment shines a light on the mountain of shame blocking your path, then shows you the way through.

We are all works in progress. We all feel shame about actions we've taken or situations we've experienced. By informing ourselves about why we feel what we feel and learning the science behind our actions and emotions, we can move through our shame and reach self-acceptance, self-assuredness, and finally, empowerment. But before we can start our journey to empowerment, we must address the mountain of shame we've spent too long ignoring. We're going to take this journey together. I've started us off, but I'll keep us rolling by telling you about the next few years of my life... when I traded in my cuddly toys for more addictive comforts.

Chapter 2

Shame: What it (Actually) is and Why We Feel it

*"Altruism is not a moral or religious ideal, no matter
what some people might tell you. It is an essential,
biological part of who or what we are as a species."*
–Bill Nye,*Undeniable: Evolution and the Science of Creation*

L ike most teenagers, my emotions weighed heavily on me,
especially my shame. Carrying intense feelings of anger,
loneliness, and shame around with me felt like balancing
pails of water across my shoulders all the time. I wanted a release.

When I was fourteen, a character on one of my favorite TV
shows, Effy from *Skins* (the UK version), dumped all of her deepest thoughts into a journal. So, I decided to start one of my own.
I used an old school notebook to lay all of my thoughts bare. I
wrote about how alone I felt. I wrote about how hopeless the world
seemed to me. I wrote about how much I wanted to die.

One day, I walked into my bedroom to unpack my bag after school, and my oldest sister was sitting on my bed. She'd come home from Uni to borrow some books from home, and while she sorted through my other sister's collection, she found my journal. She had it resting gingerly on her lap, as if it might leap up and bite her.

"I've found your notebook," she said.

My cheeks flushed with embarrassment. Those crinkled pages were filled with my deepest, darkest thoughts. But, to my surprise, a bit of hope fluttered in me too. As I watched her thumb the pages I thought, *Someone has seen it now. Someone will help me.*

I hoped my big sister might look up and tell me that my feelings were normal, that she'd felt them at my age, too. I thought at least she would come over and hug me. Instead, she watched my face for a moment, set the notebook down, got off my bed, and walked away.

Part of me hoped she'd tell my father, but she never said a word. She never mentioned the journal again. My hope deflated like an old birthday balloon. Someone had seen what was in my head and my heart, and it hadn't made a difference. Her reaction only solidified my deepest shame: *I'm the only one who feels like this. There* is *something wrong with me.*

Even though I didn't fit in with my sisters or most of my classmates, there was one person who made me feel somewhat normal when I was with her—Melanie. The more my body developed, the more Melanie seemed to tolerate me. Eventually, I felt comfortable enough to tentatively call her my friend. I was gentle about it, like she was a wild horse I could spook away with an unfunny joke or a passage from my journal. It took months for me to accept that she actually *wanted* to be my friend.

As we grew closer, Melanie trusted me with a secret. She told me how she managed to appear so well put together: she used powerful stimulants. Her effortless charm, confident demeanor, and bubbly personality were all carefully constructed facades, and they were tough for her to maintain. She felt shame about the person she projected, and drugs were her coping mechanism. It wasn't long before they became my coping mechanism, too.

The two of us ventured into all the places our parents warned us not to go—dark alleys, abandoned parking lots, strangers' homes. We met with drug dealers twenty years older than us and popped pills in their living rooms. We pooled babysitting money and waitressing tips to buy whatever we could afford. Since cocaine was too expensive, we mostly stuck with M-CAT, which is more like if cocaine was *on* cocaine. Sometimes we bought weed, sometimes we bought pills…whatever we needed to keep us high or bring us low.

Melanie and I grew closer than ever because of our shared secret. We had inside jokes about our after-school adventures. We laughed, and I finally felt like I had someone who seemed to enjoy my company, who cared about me. I felt like I had a reason to be alive. And the world felt *good.*

I wanted the feeling to last forever.

So, I got high whenever I could.

Looking back, I didn't consider what I was doing as an attempt to hide from my shame. I didn't think about shame at all—drugs have a way of taking those thoughts away from you. The brief moments I did feel shame, when my psyche managed to break through with a message about how dangerous my actions were, I quickly silenced them with a pill or a joint or a line. I suppressed my old life and embraced my new social status. I shoved my shame into the deepest corner of my mind and shrouded it in smoke.

Ignoring my shame hurt me in the long run. Shame is a necessary part of the human experience. It is a red flag waved by our brains to warn us that our behavior is in conflict with what we consider "good." It's part of our inner moral compass. So, if we're going to learn how to face our shame, then we must understand how shame actually helps us.

Shame serves a crucial function that keeps us humans alive, but it's so uncomfortable that its usefulness isn't always obvious. For some, shame gives rise to dangerous and damaging feelings of worthlessness, inferiority, and problematic behaviors. For others, shame motivates a willingness to make amends with those who have been wronged, and a desire for positive behavior change. The problem isn't the existence of shame, rather it's the way we perceive shame, our willingness to face it, our internalization of shame, and the intensity at which we feel it.

I like the way sociologist Thomas J. Scheff describes shame: it is "our moral gyroscope." Without shame, humans wouldn't be nearly as advanced as we are today. We feel shame when we don't follow our instinct to cooperate with others. Shame stops us from committing acts of violence and instead encourages us to work together. It motivates us to help others even when it inconveniences us. It convinces us to do the right thing when no one else is looking. Shame is still a part of humanity because it serves our entire species.

To understand how facing your shame will benefit you, let's break down the emotion's function into three categories:

1. Social Survival: shame helps humans progress as a cooperative species.
2. Physical Survival: shame discourages us from behaving in ways that are harmful (or at least it's supposed to).
3. Sense of Self: shame spurs us to act in ways that benefit ourselves and others (or...at least it's supposed to).

When we understand how shame functions in these capacities, it's a little less scary to face the uncomfortable feelings of the emotion.

Social Survival: Cooperation and Punishment

Humanity's survival depends on our ability to cooperate with each other. In most cases, cooperation is the easiest and most beneficial way for humans to achieve their goals. However, there are some situations in which people believe they can accomplish their goals easier alone. Shame is a tool the human brain uses as a warning signal to those who believe it's easier to operate alone. We've never functioned better alone than we have together, and a healthy dose of shame is sometimes what we need to remind us of that.

Early humans stuck together because forming groups increased their chances of survival. The primitive world was full of uncertainty and the constant presence of threats, like predators, starvation, poisonous food, injury, sickness, or all of the above limited survival odds. Establishing group cohesion and cooperation was a fundamental part of staying alive.

The more humans joined together, the higher their survival chances became. Group members could share information about what was safe to eat, where to find clean water, how to build a shelter, and how to build a fire. Hunting and gathering were easier with more people involved. Raising offspring was easier when there were enough people to split up hunting, gathering, and babysitting responsibilities.

The more humans survived in a group, the more they passed down the traits that helped them do so. Each generation of humans became better at surviving because they inherited the successful skills of their ancestors. Traits like communication, cooperation, and shame made the evolutionary cut, since they proved useful to anyone who survived long enough to pass on their genes.

Human beings are not just driven to be socially cooperative—we are genetically designed for it. From the moment we come into this world, we begin the search for who we belong with, who we are safe with, who we love, and who loves us back. The survival of newborn infants depends on the dedicated nurturing of parents and caregivers. Babies, toddlers, and small children still rely on their caregivers for food, water, shelter, warmth, and attention. Without these years of round-the-clock care and support, baby humans cannot develop into healthy adults, physically or psychologically.

This need for social closeness doesn't disappear once we learn to walk and talk on our own. We still rely on social groups long after we are strong enough to secure our own basic survival. In fact, our desire for closeness grows stronger and expands beyond our basic needs as we develop. In adolescents, for example, being accepted by one's peers is a critical factor in supporting mental wellbeing, while social rejection negatively affects mental health, physical health, and academic success. Additionally, adolescents who are liked less than their peers are at greater risk of depression.

Humans never truly outgrow the need for social bonds. For proof of this, look no further than the world's longest scientific study of adult life.[2] Dr. Robert Waldinger is the current (and the fourth) director of a Harvard University study that's been tracking the lives of 724 adult men for the last eighty-five years. Only about sixty of the men are still alive, and the study carries on through the original subjects' more than 2,000 children (of all genders). In 1938, this study began as a way to find the answer to a simple question: what is the most important component of a long, healthy life?

The researchers selected people who would grow up to experience all walks of life. There were two main pools of participants: one group consisted of white, male, juvenile delinquents from Boston. Most lived in crowded tenements, and rarely had access to basic necessities like running water. The other group consisted of white, male sophomore students at Harvard College. This broad array gave the researchers confidence in their exhaustive findings, as the young men grew to become doctors, lawyers, blue collar workers, bricklayers…and one became President of the United States.

The research group still collects as much data as possible about their subjects' lives. They conduct psychological evaluations at the subjects' homes. They collect medical records from the subjects' doctors. They take blood, MRI scans, and conduct interviews with the men, their spouses, and their children. All of this helps the researchers build the clearest possible picture of what makes these men tick.

"The clearest lesson we have from this study is this," said Dr. Waldinger in his 2015 TEDx Talk, "good relationships keep us happier and healthier…social connections are really good for us, and loneliness kills. It turns out, people who are more socially connected to family, to friends, to community are happier, they're physically healthier, and they live longer than people who are less well-connected."

By the time the first round of men in the study turned fifty, researchers could predict how their lives would unfold. The team didn't make predictions based on their cholesterol levels, but by how satisfied the subjects were in their relationships. The fifty-year-old men who reported the highest satisfaction in their relationships were the healthiest by age eighty. Their minds were sharper, their bodies functioned better, and their outlook on their lives were more positive than the lonely subjects in the study.

This study revealed a truth that humans have carried with us since our inception: social relationships protect us. They give us sanctuary and purpose at times when life is cruel. The kind of relationships (family, romantic partners, or friends) or how many relationships we maintain don't matter—it's the quality of those relationships that keep us living long, healthy lives.

Humanity's social nature is in stark contrast to our friends in the animal kingdom who are born without the need to form social groups. Most animals are born relatively self-sufficient. For example, an infant giraffe falls to the ground when birthed and is able to stand itself up within thirty minutes. These marvelous creatures are born with nervous systems and brains developed at the level of a human one-year-old. It is safe to say that human infants are not this self-sufficient from the get-go.

While other animals are born ready to run from predators and gather their own meals, humans have evolved beyond the need to start out self-sufficient. The time we spend growing and developing gives our brains time to reach their full complexity. Since humans rely on each other to survive, our brains have adapted to function best when cooperating with others.

The human brain is one of the most complicated systems in the known universe. Being able to explore the different neural circuits associated with social functioning is a scientific marvel. Over years of studies and research, scientists have determined a surprisingly strong connection inside of the brain's reward system. The reward system extends from the striatum (the motor and reward handout system) to the ventromedial prefrontal cortex (decision-making and emotional regulation systems).[3] This means we value rewards based on more than how they keep us alive: we also value them based on how they make us feel.

Non-social rewards, like food, money, or goods, are obviously valuable because they keep us alive. Social rewards, like a gift from someone else, also activates our neural reward system and makes us feel good. However, this same system is also active when we perceive an interaction to be socially rewarding, and when we are cooperating. Pleasant conversation, fun social gatherings, and bonding experiences are equally as valuable to our brains as a box of chocolates, a crisp $20 bill, or even a warm place to sleep.

Studies have shown that when individuals cooperate with others and expect cooperation in return, their brain's reward system shows increased activity. The spike occurs before the other person has a chance to choose cooperation—even the simple act of anticipating cooperation gets us excited! However, if that same individual doesn't expect the other person to be cooperative, there is no activation, not until after the other person actually shows cooperation. In those cases, we only feel rewarded when cooperation is mutual.

There is always a risk of being exploited when we cooperate with others. However, studies like the one mentioned above still show that mutual cooperation is not only the most satisfying and mentally rewarding outcome, it's also the only outcome neurologically perceived as rewarding. We are naturally driven to assume others are likely to be cooperative, and that is why, for most of us, cooperation is the first strategy we choose when given the option.

Because society depends on the naturally social and cooperative human, there are regulations in place to discourage those who are non-cooperators. Sometimes, people are willing to take advantage of others' natural inclination toward cooperation and prosocial behavior. This is where punishment, both internal and external, comes into play.

Part of cooperation is maintaining a sense of fairness and trust. When these bonds are broken in a human social group, there must be consequences for the ones who broke them, or the group will crumble. The other members of the social group may decide to punish the transgressors. Internally, negative emotions like guilt, shame, and embarrassment punish the transgressors for acting in ways that threaten their place within the group.

Humans are not only driven to punish those that act unfairly toward others—we are willing to punish them even when doing so doesn't benefit us directly, or even when it costs us. This is known as altruistic punishment. Research has shown that cooperation works best in groups where altruistic punishment is possible, and groups without it break down.

Why are we willing to put ourselves in harm's way to make sure others are punished? It turns out, we find altruistic punishment as rewarding as cooperation. The same areas in our brain respond positively when we see others follow the rules as it does when we see them punished for breaking the rules. A group of researchers from the University of Zurich figured this out by designing the perfect storm for altruistic punishment: online video games.[4]

For this study, two volunteers sat down to play an online game with an anonymous partner. Both players knew they faced another human (not a computer.) For simplicity, we're going to name the players Anne and Bill. This is how the game worked: Anne and Bill each receive 10 "money units," which we'll call coins, at the start of the game. Anne goes first, and she has a choice to make: she can either send 10 coins to Bill or keep her 10 coins. Anne knows if she sends the coins to Bill, the game quadruples her deposit and gives

Bill 40 coins total. If she keeps them, nothing happens, and both players go home with 10 coins.

Anne sends the coins to Bill—now Bill has 50 coins and Anne has none. Bill can now choose to either send Anne half of the pot, 25 coins, or keep the full 50 for himself. If Bill acts trustworthily and sends back half, both players earn 25 coins, but if Bill keeps all the money, he earns 50 coins and Anne, who trusted Bill, earns nothing.

This experiment hypothesized that if Anne trusts Bill, cooperation and fairness become the norms that help Bill decide to send back half the money. If Bill is untrustworthy and keeps it all, he violates an established norm, which experimenters believed would trigger Anne to wish to punish Bill…and that's where the experiment's twist came into play.

After Anne is told how Bill acts on his turn, she has one minute to decide whether she wants to punish Bill. Both players get an extra 20 coins, which allows Anne to finance this punishment if she chooses to go through with it. She can spend up to 20 coins to assign Bill "punishment points" that take away his coins. Each punishment point takes away 2 of Bill's coins, but it also costs Anne 1 coin per point. If she doesn't punish Bill, Anne and Bill each walk away with their winnings—Anne with 20 coins and Bill with 70 coins.

During her one minute of deliberation, Anne's brain was monitored with a positron emission tomography (PET) scan. Anne's brain revealed that when she thought about punishing Bill for acting untrustworthy, the thought provided relief to her feelings of betrayal, which activated the reward center in her brain. In fact, in subsequent iterations of the test, when the first player and the second player cooperated, their brains activated in a similar fashion to Anne and Bill. This tells us that humans find cooperation rewarding, but when we feel someone has acted unfairly toward us or someone else, we also find it rewarding to punish them.

Now, cheating at a game is a pretty low-stakes crime to commit against a social group, but this transgression still functions as a broken rule. Our brains know their best chance (and therefore our best chance) at survival is to cooperate with others and make connections in social groups. That means playing by the rules, cooperating with others, and presenting positive behaviors. If we deviate from the established rules, or "norms" of our groups, our brains send out warning signals to let us know we're in danger of being punished, or even removed.

As the human race expanded across the world, different cultures emerged with their own established sets of rules and norms. As survival became easier, new social expectations appeared. Fitting into a community became less about survival skills focused on other contributions, like homemaking, breadwinning, and property ownership.

These more intricate social groups brought new struggles for people to overcome to stay in their social group. Staying alive wasn't enough to secure your spot—there was a whole new set of expectations to meet. And if you deviated outside of them, you were considered strange, or worse, unfit.

This is still true today. In the US, the complex cultural standards tend to leave most people feeling like they don't fit in. For example, there are still some antiquated standards in place around the nuclear family. If you are a woman over 30, you are expected to have children. If your partner works full time, you are expected to stay home with the kids. As a man, you are expected to earn the majority of the household income to protect and provide for your family.

I'm a woman in my mid-20s (at the time of writing this) and I'm still single. I often joke that I'm married to my career, because I find it hard to believe any person can bring me the same joy and fulfillment. I have no interest in having kids, but I'm often told by other people—especially older men—that I *do* actually want children, I just don't know it yet. I've bumped into women at conferences and events who stopped to tell me how they used to be like me, thinking they didn't want kids, until they met the man of their dreams and they realized, deep down, they wanted children all along.

"It'll happen to you!" they tell me, toting a wagon full of sticky fingers and runny noses behind them, "Just wait until that biological clock starts ticking!"

These are examples of other humans leveraging social shame for the good of the species. Will my behavior ever change? I don't know. I'm fairly content with where I am in my life and my career right now, but I can't see the future any more than the next person can. There's no arguing, though, that it *should* be in the best interest of the species for as many people to procreate as possible. That's not to say that everyone should, but it helps single people like me to understand that humans have evolved to shame non-conformers as a survival mechanism, and it's not personal.

Physical Survival: Stress and Isolation

We do all we can to assure our social relationships are strong because isolation is painful. The pain reaches further than the figurative language we use to describe it, like a broken heart or an empty chest. When we go through life alone, we're physically damaged by a lack of social bonds.

Researchers have known for a long time that our social relationships are important for our wellbeing. There is a mountain of evidence that social relationships keep us alive, help us cope with our daily stressors, and make us happy, but over the last few decades more research has focused on the negative side of social relationships: what happens when they *don't* form.

Sometimes, feeling shame causes people to isolate themselves instead of seeking social support. It's a vicious cycle—when you feel ashamed, you feel like a bad person worthy of judgment. Rather than reach out for support or guidance, you may prefer to withdraw or "disappear" altogether to avoid any judgment at all.

Given the impact of close social relationships on our wellbeing, isolating yourself from others when you feel shame is an unhealthy choice. Social isolation exacerbates issues like depression, loneliness, poor sleep quality, and cognitive impairment, each of which reduces your emotional coping ability and quality of life.

The risks of social isolation were thrown into the spotlight during the COVID-19 pandemic. All around the world, people were isolated from their families, friends, and everyone else. Even small interactions with coffee shop baristas or checkout workers were kept to a minimum. People who once held rich, healthy social lives were shoved into their homes and told to stay put. Some people didn't see another soul for weeks at a time.

In a 2015 study, psychology researchers detailed the dangers of social isolation and loneliness.[5] A person who lacks social connections faces the same health risks as someone who smokes fifteen cigarettes a day. Loneliness and isolation are twice as harmful to physical and mental health as obesity. Social bonds may not immediately appear to be crucial for survival, but a life lived alone can end much earlier than you'd expect.

It may seem obvious that individuals who struggle to form social connections are less capable of coping with mental struggles, but it turns out they're also less likely to cope well with physical struggles too. A lack of social interaction increases levels of chronic stress, which can wreak havoc on the human body and cause physical issues.

Falling short of expectations is stressful, whether they come from you or your culture. A person's identity within the context of their social group plays a large role in their self-esteem and sense of belonging. Falling short of those expectations can cause stress, especially when underachieving could mean losing your social standing.

When humans experience stress, our bodies flood with cortisol. Cortisol is the stress hormone. Cortisol is like our body's first responder—it is first to arrive on the scene when there might be danger, ready to propel us into a fight or help us run away. In order to get us into action, cortisol first shuts down some of the body's less important systems so it can focus on responding to the stress or danger more efficiently; this is a lifesaving role, and we need this in times of danger. However, the problem with cortisol is that when it is released in abundance for too long, the effects stop becoming life-saving and start becoming life threatening.

When cortisol floods through your system, you feel it take over. Your heart beats heavy in your chest as your blood pumps harder and faster. Your body grows hot, you might experience some dizziness or shaking as your body prepares to run. You might feel sick to your stomach, since cortisol shuts down your digestive system to reroute all of your energy into surviving whatever is stressing you out.

The human body's stress response works wonders in moments of immediate danger, but some stress lasts longer than a moment. Problems arise when stress levels stay high for long periods of time. Cortisol keeps vital systems suppressed or shut down, and we stop functioning as well.

One of the systems that cortisol shuts down during stressful periods is the immune system—the body's natural defense against germs, viruses, and more. When stress spikes for a short period of time, the immune system isn't considered vital. What are the odds you'll come in contact with a virus in the time it takes you to throw a punch or run for cover? However, without your immune system functioning at full capacity, you're left vulnerable for longer periods of time and your risk of exposure rises. You're left susceptible to a spectrum of diseases and illnesses, starting with a cold or flu, and reaching all the way to cancers, heart disease, and digestive diseases.

Avoiding this kind of pain means valuing social relationships in a healthy way. During my time with Melanie, I overcorrected and placed too much value in our friendship. The rewards I felt when I spent time with her outweighed the damage I did to my body. I didn't care about my relationships with my parents, my sisters, or myself, because none of those proved as rewarding as this one. I finally had a friend, someone who valued me, who *chose* me, and I wasn't keen on giving that up. Any time I felt shame about the drugs I did, the schoolwork I missed, or the rules I broke at home, I quickly dismissed it; fixing those problems wasn't worth losing my friend.

What I didn't realize then was that I placed all of my self-worth into how others saw me. I poured myself out to make room for the boys who paid me attention, the classmates who envied my new social status, and my persona as a toughened teen. By the time I realized how far I'd strayed from who I wanted to be, I was too lost to find my way back.

Sense of Self: Shame as a Moral Compass

Shame isn't only an emotion felt at times when your actions put your social standing in danger; it also appears when your actions contradict your self-image. In this way, shame helps you understand who you are. Shame acts as a moral compass that helps you recognize when you've strayed too far from the path to becoming the person you want to be.

If shame is an emotion that appears when you act outside of your self-perception, that must mean you understand who you are at your essence, right?

Well, not exactly.

To better understand how shame influences the self, you must first understand the basics of The Self as a concept. This doesn't mean veering into the philosophy of what The Self is at its essence—hundreds of years of experts still haven't reached an agreement there, and I'm not about to weigh in. Rather, for the purposes of understanding The Self's relationship to shame, it's good to nail down exactly what it means to refer to "self" in terms like self-awareness, self-confidence, self-empowerment, and self-esteem.

Definitions for The Self change depending on who you ask. Sociologists consider The Self as a socially constructed mental image of who a person is across contexts, accumulated through social relationships and socializations. They consider The Self as a separate entity from identity; The Self stays stable across varying contexts, but identities can change based on the groups we belong to. Every person may harbor many identities, but each only has one true Self.

Psychologists are notoriously fascinated by this notion of an underlying true Self, as well as our awareness or unawareness of it. They believe we all have a true sense of self within us, regardless of how well we recognize it. On the other hand, if you ask a neuro-scientist, they might tell you The Self is a collection of information from different memory systems. In other words, our sense of who we are stems from the intricate retrieval of information from different memory systems, including memories of previous experiences, behaviors, and emotions.

Even if you're not able to paint the perfect picture of what your Self looks like, you probably have some notion of who you are—or who you'd like to be. Would you rather spend a weekend partying with friends or curled up with a book? Are you the type to turn in the wallet you found in a parking lot, or keep the cash inside? Are you a dog person, a cat person, or a lizard person? These are all small questions, but their answers stack on top of each other to form the vague shape of your sense of self.

Asking these sorts of questions and finding the shape of your-self is an act of self-reflection. Self-reflection is not just entirely about the individual; it benefits everyone around you, particularly those you are closest to. When you become more aware of yourself through self-reflection, you are better equipped for positive social relationships. You are more likely to show positive traits like kind-ness, empathy, and cooperation.

Understanding who you are is crucial for coping with feelings like shame and guilt. Sharp stings from rising shame might feel like your body is rebelling against you if you're not sure where the feel-ing is coming from. However, once you understand the foundation of who you are, you're better equipped to recognize how far your choices have carried you from that foundation, and you can more easily make your way back to base.

Running from your shame is a quick way to lose your sense of self. If you're spending too much time in flight mode, making quick decisions that don't always align with who you are, it won't be long before you realize you've run right into a dead end. Out-running your shame only suppresses it in the short term—it won't be long before it overwhelms you and causes more harm to your self-image, your self-esteem, and your ability to grow into the person you want to be.

Chapter 3

Why We Suppress Shame
(And Why That Hurts Us)

*"Our doubts are traitors, and make us lose the good
we might oft win, by fearing to attempt."*
–William Shakespeare, *Measure for Measure*

O n my sixteenth birthday, Dad agreed to let me host
a party. I suspect he was relieved to hear me ask.
Finally, he must have thought, *Abbie's making friends
and fitting in!* Of course, he had no idea how dangerous my
friends were.

Dad and I spent weeks preparing for this party. He helped me
design a menu, decorate the house, and send out invitations. All of
my friends RSVP'd yes. On the day of the party, Dad graciously
stepped out of the house to let us hang out in peace. In his mind, the
worst trouble we could manage was taking the bottle of schnapps
out of the liquor cabinet.

He returned to a nightmare scene that evening. My friends brought their friends, who brought their friends, and by the time my dad came home, I only knew half the people in his living room. Guests were draped across his furniture like throw blankets. White powder covered every surface like a thick layer of dust. He walked in just as I was finishing a line myself. We made eye contact then, and his face contorted into a series of emotions—disappointment, fear, and finally, anger.

My dad threw everyone out of the house. My friends shuffled out with dazed expressions, their arms full of bongs and bottles. When the house was mostly empty, my dad turned and walked out the door, too. He left to spend the night at his girlfriend's house. He didn't stay to make sure I followed orders or, more importantly, stayed safe.

My first thought was that he didn't care, but I soon realized it was more likely he couldn't bear to look at me. Still, with the house empty of adults once again, the few friends who stayed behind to help "clean up" were free to finish up the drugs left behind with me.

Once the drugs wore off, I felt my shame rising like an incoming tide. I knew it would drown me if I didn't start running. Just as I was ready to leave my friends at home to tear off in an unknown direction, the doorbell rang.

It was Danny, a guy I'd heard of before but met officially at my party. He'd come back to help clean up. Danny joined the rest of my stragglers on the sofa, and we exchanged stories and gossip until the sun came up.

Life at home was tough in the weeks after the party. Summer melted into fall, and I still hadn't shared more than a few words with my dad. When he finally decided to speak to me again, he couldn't help but shout at me. I spent most evenings closed behind my bedroom door. Then, at night, I snuck out to meet Danny, and we numbed ourselves with drugs and daydreamed about a different life. Sometimes he'd take me along to some of his deals—he sold drugs, too. He'd bring me back to the curb outside just as the sun's first light streaked across the sky. Then I'd do it all again the next day.

Danny was a much-needed escape from the tension at home. I liked spending time with him, but he was interested in getting to know the "real me" underneath the messy party girl. I wasn't sure I had much more to show him.

One afternoon, I asked him if he wanted to go to a party, and he told me he'd rather stay in and watch a movie.

"It could be like a date," he said.

"We never do stuff like that," I said.

"Yeah, but we could."

Later that night, I showed up at his house with two of my friends. We were all wasted. He opened the door and we all stumbled inside, brushing past his confused, annoyed expression. My friends spilled over his couch and turned on the TV. I went to join them, but Danny stopped me. He motioned for me to follow him upstairs.

I nodded woozily and headed for his bedroom. Before I could even sit down on his bed, he started in on me.

"What are you doing?" he demanded.

"What?" I said, wobbling a little, "we're going out, right?"

"No, I thought we were going to watch a movie."

I waved a hand at him. "Oh, no, that's...I don't want to do that."

He didn't say anything. I tried to read his emotions from his expression, but I couldn't focus on his face. My vision was swimming and swirling around, making it too hard to see much of anything.

"We can watch a movie," I tried, hoping to stop an argument.

"Why did you bring your friends here?" he said after a moment.

I went to answer him, but I didn't really know what to say. I hadn't forgotten he wanted to watch a movie. I knew he wanted to have a nice night alone with me. I couldn't place where it came from, but something inside of me recoiled at the idea of closeness with Danny. He wanted to see the real me, but even I wasn't sure what she looked like. Was she anything more than a shy, bookish girl with a backpack full of stuffies? Did she even *exist* anymore?

"I think…I—"

I couldn't finish talking. My vision tunneled. I tried to sit, but it was too late. Everything went black.

I woke up on Danny's floor. He was pacing around my body in a panic. He looked down at me and saw I was awake. Relief rushed over his face, which was sharper now.

"What happened? What's wrong?" I asked, my words still a little slurred.

"What do you mean? You passed out right in front of me!" he said.

"Oh…I'm thorry." I touched my fingers to my tongue. It was swollen and a little sore. Danny saw me reach for my mouth.

"Yeah, you started choking on your tongue. I had to hold it out of the way. I've had my finger down your throat trying to keep you breathing."

As my clarity came back, I realized Danny was shaken. I'd scared him.

"I'm sorry," I said again, mindful of my swollen tongue.

"Just…you can stay up here for a bit and sober up, okay? But after that, you guys have to leave. I can't deal with…" he waved his arms around me, "all this. It's too much of a mess."

I nodded and he headed back downstairs. I took a few minutes to collect myself. My friends and I left, and that was one of the last times I saw Danny.

I was alone again. Even at home, I couldn't seem to reconcile with my dad. My older sister was off at university and my younger sister wasn't interested in spending time with me. I hated every moment I was by myself, so I spent as much time as possible out with my friends. I didn't try to hide the drugs or drinking from my dad anymore. Why should I? It wasn't like anyone cared.

My dad couldn't take my behavior anymore and kicked me out. He sent me to my mum, who agreed to let me move in as long as I followed the "seen but not heard" rule. She would let me stay, but I wasn't to expect anything from her. Weeks with her turned to months, and there was nothing left of the old Abbie. My grades plummeted. My mum avoided me. I was back to being the piggy in the middle, and it felt like everyone around me tried their hardest to stay away. Meanwhile, every moment I spent alone, I heard the rush of my shame as it creeped closer.

The last leaves dropped from the trees outside and frost framed the windows of my mum's house. Since she wasn't interested in my whereabouts, I didn't have to sneak around at all hours of the night anymore. I spent most of my time off at parties. Sometimes I knew the people. Sometimes I didn't.

When my mum told me she and her fiancé were leaving for a New Years' Eve party, I decided it was time for me to redeem myself with my friends. I took Mum's absence as an opportunity to throw a New Years' Eve party of my own. Not long after she left for the night, the house was teeming with teens under the influence of everything under the sun.

With Danny's voice circling in my head, I had made the conscious decision not to take drugs at this party. Someone else, though, decided to take that choice from me by spiking my drink. Before I knew it, I was gone.

I remember chatting with some friends, then waking up on the floor of my Mum's spare room to her screaming at me in front of a gaggle of police officers. A neighbor called the police to complain about the noise…and about the pile of furniture stacked on the lawn like a barricade. I had no clue how that happened. The house was almost empty, save a few plastic red cups and piles of glass from broken windows.

This time Mum grounded me, but she quickly lost interest in enforcing the punishment. It wasn't a week before I was back out partying again. I slipped deeper into my own denial. I deluded myself into thinking I was totally in control of my actions. The damage I'd done to my relationships, my school records, and my body didn't register with me. I was a black hole, and I had no interest in exploring my own devastation.

I wasn't even at rock bottom yet, and I was already suppressing most of my shame.

It feels impossible to face shame before you're ready. Processing shame is uncomfortable, but if you suppress your shame and live in denial, you put yourself in danger. You leave room for maladaptive behavior patterns that take you away from a healthy self-image and a sense of true empowerment. And that's what was happening to me.

The human brain is a master at keeping itself alive, even if that means protecting itself from you. When you experience an adrenaline rush in response to a physical threat, it's because your brain triggered a series of actions to help you take on danger. When you face mental or emotional threats, your brain is also prepared to protect you…even if that means shutting your consciousness out.

In some cases, it actually *is* impossible to face shame before you're ready. If you don't have healthy coping mechanisms for handling shame, guilt, embarrassment, or other negative emotions, your brain can stop you from experiencing those emotions temporarily. It's like your brain tosses the memory into a box, locks it up, and tucks it away until it believes you can address it safely.

It can be comforting to keep your most painful thoughts and feelings locked away in a box in the back of your mind, far away from conscious thought or analysis. The thought of opening that box, looking directly at yourself—at your behaviors—is unnerving. It's a much more pleasant option to delude yourself into believing you've already opened the box and dealt with its contents. It's easier to pretend there is no box, or that the box isn't a problem anymore.

Suppression is generally considered to be a bad thing, but that's not always the case. Sometimes our brains have good reasons for suppressing memories. Suppression can free up the brain's capacity to find a safe place to reflect. However, when it is time to reflect, suppression gets in the way. And this becomes a problem if we're going to face shame, become more resilient, and discover a new sense of empowerment.

To overcome the urge to suppress shame, it helps to know what suppression is and how it works. It will also help to know what suppression is not—I find there is often confusion between "suppression" and "repression," so I will clear that up. Then, I'll break down the two specific ways suppression gets in the way of our ability to face shame: by stopping our self-reflection and by stopping our regulation. When we understand what we're up against, we can calmly move past it to the point where we are ready to face the deeper, harder memories at the core of our shame.

Suppression, Not Repression

Your brain knows you better than you know yourself…literally. If there are memories from your past your brain thinks you cannot process without harming yourself physically, mentally, or emotionally, it will protect you from those memories. This process is called suppression.

Despite popular belief, the notion that we can repress memories, meaning they are completely forgotten, is heavily contradicted by current scientific understanding. We can, however, suppress memories and emotions for a while. Our brains can take painful memories and file them away, keeping them safe and away from our immediate attention, until we're ready to face them.

Repression implies that painful memories are tucked so far away from your conscious mind that they will never resurface without serious effort. But that's not quite what happens. Painful memories don't leave, but your brain can tuck them back into less visible corners of your mind until it decides you're ready to process what happened. These memories are not invisible, though, nor are they ever truly out of reach. They can still leak out of that box and influence your behaviors without you realizing it.

In addition to suppressing memories, the brain can also suppress emotions. This is helpful in emergency situations—when your house is on fire, your brain pushes away your sadness until you and your loved ones are safe outside. However, the human brain hasn't evolved well enough to tell the difference between a life-threatening emergency, like a fire, and a wellbeing-threatening emergency, like a deadline at the end of the week. Your brain will suppress emotions to help you clear the threat, then deal with the emotions later. But this isn't always the ideal path for handling mental struggles.

When you are under increased stress, suppressed emotions and memories can manifest in your behavior, even without your conscious awareness. Let's look at an example: say a friend of yours gets a puppy and invites you over to meet him. You head over and see the most adorable little Rottweiler puppy you've ever seen. You give him lots of snuggles, kisses, and you play ball with him until he's tuckered out. You thank your friend and head back home, feeling warmed by the interaction.

The next time you visit your friend, that Rottweiler is a full-blown, 125-pound dog. He sees you from across the yard and bounds toward you with excitement. You're not sure why, but your heart starts pounding in your chest. You break out in a cold sweat. Your breathing hitches and you flinch as he comes closer. You give him plenty of pets and love, but your hands are shaking. You can't help feeling nervous around him. You're confused by your reaction—you've already met him! You loved him last time! Why does he seem so scary now, when he's never given you a reason for concern?

You mention this interaction to your mom next time you see her, and her face falls. She reminds you that when you were little, your neighbors had a Rottweiler chained out back in their yard. She broke loose one day after a nasty storm and you found her hiding under your porch. When you tried to pull her out, she bit you on the forearm and you ended up in the hospital.

You look down and see, sure enough, a faint white line tracing up your forearm. *How did I forget about that?* You think to yourself, but you don't say it out loud. Instead, you feel a sense of shame rising up in your chest. *I love dogs,* you think, but now that sentence sends a faint sting up your arm. A blurry memory of a wet, muddy Rottie with wild eyes appears in your mind.

You've always known yourself to be an animal lover, despite this one incident. Your brain also knows you to be an animal lover, so it tucked away a memory that could cause a confusing contradiction in your mind. Now, as an adult, you recognize that dog wasn't at fault for her behavior. She was scared, and probably hurt, too. However, if you'd processed that experience as a child, you might not love animals as much as you do now. You have years of experience with all kinds of household pets to solidify yourself as an animal lover now, which helps you process your early trauma and work through this unconscious fear of big dogs.

Suppression can be helpful in this way—it can stop you from facing hard memories until you're distanced enough from them to process them healthily. However, suppression is mentally exhausting. Without a healthy self-introspection process, your brain spends too much energy on suppressing shameful memories and emotions, and those memories are more likely to leak out in unexpected ways.

In 2017, a group of researchers collected eighty-eight couples who had been together for at least three months.[6] Each couple watched an emotionally disturbing clip from a World War II documentary, then discussed the contents together. But this experiment wasn't designed to help the couples bond over a shared emotional experience. Instead, researchers encouraged one half of the couples to freely share their reaction to the footage. The other half, though, were given different instructions:

"During the conversation, behave in such a way that your partner does not know you are feeling any emotions at all. That is, try not to express your emotions outwardly. Keep stoic even when speaking about your feelings…talk about your emotions and thoughts related to the content of the video clip, but keep your face and body emotionless."

As these couples shared their reactions to the video, an unnerving dynamic arose. Partners who shared their emotions freely and were met with stoic, unfeeling responses showed signs of stress: higher blood pressure, faster heartbeats, and raised cortisol levels. These participants not only noticed their partners' lack of emotional response—they were unnerved by it.

Not only is emotional suppression psychologically uncomfortable for us, it's uncomfortable for those around us, too. This study showed the significance of suppressing emotions in social contexts. When you suppress emotions, the people you interact with can identify the suppression and may feel uncomfortable, or even threatened. To put it simply, suppressing emotions makes you a worse communicator.

Everyone has had days where nothing went right, but nothing felt wrong enough to merit complaining. Your morning was a series of disappointing coffee, stale muffins, and a pile of gum on the sidewalk. Your day at work was exhausting. Your commute felt endless. Your mind raced all day to keep track of your upcoming responsibilities. You kept a brave face for most of the day, but when you went home, all it took was a single hug to open the floodgates. Your barrier came crashing down because the act of holding it up was too difficult.

This emotional barrier is a form of suppression, and it's also a barrier to self-reflection. Sometimes the barriers people build are simply that: a wall to protect from feelings about ourselves and our experiences. Other times, the barriers we build protect us from any contradictions to how we believe the world should be and how we should feel. In other words, we want to perceive ourselves more positively, and we want to believe that the world is in line with our belief systems and expectations; when it's not, we warp our perspectives.

Most of the time we don't even know why we hold the beliefs that we do, yet we are still highly resistant to any information to the contrary. When we're in a healthy mental state, we approach contradictory information through introspection. However, if we're stuck in a state of suppression, we're not likely to face those contradictions with logic, reason, or an open mind.

Suppressing Shame Stops Introspection

Scientists believe—though it's impossible to say for sure—that humans are one of the only species on Earth that can engage in introspection. Some people's first instinct is to argue that shame is an unwanted side effect of reflective intelligence, but that argument diminishes shame's role in our species' evolutionary history. Shame is a key component of motivating self-improvement, signaling that we must learn and grow through our experiences. The problem is that we have an extraordinary number of barriers and limitations to our self-reflective ability. The first step to knowing yourself is recognizing those barriers and limits so you can address them in a healthy way.

Our species is unique in our ability to contemplate our own thoughts, feelings, and place in the social world. When we are living up to our own expectations, self-reflection can be empowering. It feels good to reflect on accomplishments, healthy relationships, and personal growth. But self-reflection doesn't always result in self-praise. Sometimes we don't like the person who looks back at us, and with that comes shame.

Suppressing shame for long periods of time is harmful. A lack of self-awareness as a result of suppression or avoidance is associated with unhealthy behaviors and habits, unhealthy and toxic relationships, poor mental and physical health, and reduced productivity and motivation.[7] Some people avoid their shame by drinking and doing drugs. Others remove the possibility of self-reflection by spending all of their time with other people, so they're never alone with their thoughts. Some people eat too much. Some don't eat at all. Some run into the arms or the beds of bad influences. Some even hide inside themselves, disengaging from the world and isolating themselves from others.

Everyone uses different coping mechanisms, but they all reach the same endpoint: a painful confrontation with shame. If you keep running from your growing shame, one day, you'll turn around to see a mountain. I've experienced my own mountain of shame. I've also spoken with others who have experienced the same overwhelming confrontation with shame by waiting too long to address it.

I've spoken with members of rehab facilities who admitted suppressing their shame made their recovery harder. Patients, staff, and even ex-patients who became staff shared their stories with me. There is a common pattern that appeared, both with individuals in rehab and those who participate in Alcoholics Anonymous and Narcotics Anonymous meetings. Recovering addicts often admit they had trouble facing the shame of what they did. So, they kept engaging in the same behaviors to avoid self-confrontation.

Most people are guilty of suppressing their shame with avoidance. On a small scale, this avoidance appears when people procrastinate finishing a daunting task, like cleaning at home or pushing off a project at work. On a larger scale, avoidance can look like tiptoeing around a hard conversation with a loved one, or ignoring responsibilities at home or work altogether.

One individual, a man who was five years clean of drugs and alcohol, told me this:

"My shame was piling up behind me. It was making a mess out of my life and I couldn't turn around to face it. I felt like my only option was to keep running and piling up my mistakes behind me while I ran. Eventually, I had to face myself. And it was the hardest thing I ever did, looking at myself like that. Everything inside of me was telling me to hide. But I needed my life back. I needed to turn around and face it so I could salvage what was left of myself."

When addicts recover from their addictions, whether they're addicted to drugs, alcohol, food, video games, or more, their first step is to stop running from their shame. That's why the first step in the 12-Step Recovery program is admitting there is a problem. It's the first moment of introspection, which in turn creates an opportunity to face shame. That first step forces people to stop in their tracks, turn around, and say, "I have a problem. I can't solve it while I'm running. I have to stop. I have to reflect."

Suppressing Shame Stops Regulation

It's hard for shame to function as our moral compass if we ignore or suppress it. By discouraging selfish behaviors, shame motivates prosocial interpersonal behaviors. Shame signals a threat to our social bonds and helps us maintain relationships.

Shame plays a role in the recognition and regulation of all other emotions. If you feel overjoyed, fearful, or angry but are ashamed of that emotion in that context, it is a signal that the emotion may be socially or morally inappropriate. Anyone who has ever felt the urge to laugh at a funeral or sob uncontrollably at a wedding will be familiar with this kind of emotional regulation.

When you feel a twinge of shame about your reaction, you're likely to suppress that emotion to maintain social norms. If you choose to suppress the shame response instead, you're probably going to receive some nasty looks from the people around you. Your social status will be damaged because you broke social norms. By acknowledging and addressing your shame, you use it as a tool to keep you in check, and steer yourself away from any moral transgressions.

Emotions are at the core of human behavior and our experiences of the world. They can be beautiful or overwhelming, and they're not always logical. Emotional regulation stops us from lashing out when our emotions threaten to overwhelm us.

Suppressing shame stops people from growing emotionally intelligent. Without shame, humans would have a more difficult time regulating their emotions. When we're angry, when we're sad, or even when we're feeling giddy, a healthy sense of emotional regulation stops us from inflicting our emotional experience on others. It stops us from screaming at people, bringing them down, or annoying them with mismatched energy. If we're not emotionally intelligent enough to regulate ourselves, our emotions take control of our actions.

People who have difficulty regulating their emotions are more likely to engage in dangerous behaviors like substance abuse, problem drinking, self-harm, high-risk sexual choices, eating disorders, and more. Difficulty self-regulating emotions leads to difficulty self-regulating the behaviors caused by those emotions running rampant. Then, when you start engaging in those dangerous behaviors, your shame builds. And the shame you feel compounds on the original shame. This new shame feels like too much to face, so you deny it. You keep self-destructing. Now you're locked in a vicious cycle.

When you're in the throes of this shame cycle, it feels like you've been running too long to look back now. You might realize you're engaging in unhealthy behaviors—maybe your studies are slipping, or you're making poor choices in friends or sexual partners. So, you tell yourself, *I just need to get those grades up,* or, *I just need to raise my standards a bit, then everything will be okay.* But that's not true. It won't be okay, because it's not the behavior that's the problem—it's a symptom, not the cause. The shame you're avoiding is the cause.

It's human nature to want to address the surface-level behaviors as they appear instead of the underlying issue. That's why Whack-A-Mole can be such an addicting game. It's so satisfying when the hammer hits the stuffy little head as it pops out of the hole. But in reality, the problem isn't whether or not we can whack the mole—it's the existence of the moles in the first place. For us to begin healing from our shame, our traumas, and our emotional baggage, we must exterminate the whole molehill before it becomes a mountain. We need to start dealing with the memories and emotions we've experienced.

Your shame may seem like a barrier between where you are now and your healing journey, but you can overcome it with the right tools. Each time you suppress or deny shame, you move further away from healing. So, the first act we must take is to plant our feet, face our shame, and start the journey. It's time to move through shame and start the journey to empowerment.

Chapter 4
Shame from Trauma

"We can judge our progress by the courage of our questions and the depth of our answers, our willingness to embrace what is true rather than what feels good."
–Carl Sagan

While most of the shame we humans experience is a result of our own actions, sometimes we feel shame because of what other people have done to us. I'm not talking about secondhand embarrassment or guilt by association, though. I'm referring to shame that arises from trauma. We feel this shame when another person acts so far outside of what most consider moral that our reactions don't reflect who we want to be.

Shame from trauma is difficult to overcome. Feelings of guilt, self-consciousness, and self-worth tangle up with fear, anger, and grief. Untangling these emotions is painful. Finding their roots and addressing them feels almost impossible. But if you hope to reach a place of true empowerment, the only way to recover from trauma and shame is to move through it.

From this point on, this chapter is going to cover content some readers may find uncomfortable or upsetting. The next section contains descriptions of sexual assault and assault-related trauma, including post-traumatic experiences. If you prefer not to read this content, continue to the final section of this chapter.

There is bad in the world. There are people who have no interest in following social norms or appeasing others. Your parents warn you about them your whole life, especially if you're a woman. They warn you about the men lurking in dark alleys, the strangers who follow you back to your car. These are the people you must avoid, and if they hurt you, it's not your fault. You are a victim then, and there is no reason to be ashamed. You're simply a casualty to the badness out there.

I wasn't raped by a stranger in an alley. No one caught me and dragged me off the street. The man who raped me was someone I knew, and someone I trusted.

I won't be identifying him, or sharing anything that might suggest his identity. All anyone needs to know is that he was someone I loved. I didn't see any bad in him before he attacked me. In fact, I believed he was my safe haven. When the rest of the world felt too heavy, he was my protection.

It took me years to even use the right word to describe what happened. When I was twenty years old, I was raped. For years following the rape, my existence was shrouded in deep, woundlike shame. I felt like it was my fault for trusting, my fault for freezing, my fault for letting it happen. After a few days passed, I felt so strongly that I was at fault that I apologized to him. I told him I didn't mean to make him think I didn't want it.

But I never wanted him to do what he did to me.

I remember him pinning me down.

I remember crying.

I remember begging him to get off me while I laid helpless beneath him.

I remember the shock I felt when he stayed on top of me anyway.

For years, when I allowed the thought of that night to creep in, I felt more shame for *my* actions than anger or sadness for his. I was ashamed of freezing. I was ashamed I didn't throw him off, throw him out, or try to throw him in jail. I felt a deep, rattling betrayal at some vague space inside of me. I wanted to scream at my own brain, *Why didn't I just fight back?*

Tragically, my experience is not unique. Documented reports of victim statements have shown that victims themselves often state the same sentiment. They feel their sense of helplessness and lack of control was more psychologically damaging than the attack itself. What's more, when a victim feels they didn't do enough to stop the attack, it can even manifest into them believing they allowed it to happen. So, in the wake of such a traumatic experience, the afterthoughts can be just as damaging (if not more so) than the event itself.

Trauma is not a singular occurrence; the trauma isn't over when the traumatic event ends. Trauma burrows in and creates a home deep in your chest. No matter how much time passes, there are moments when the trauma will remind you of its presence with a cold, hollow ache. Painful memories and physical sensations associated with the trauma linger for a long time, and in some cases, they linger for a lifetime.

In my line of work, I've spoken directly with other victims of sexual assault. The questions I've been asked break my heart.

"Was it my fault?"

"Was I too weak?"

"Did I deserve it?"

"Why didn't I *do something*?"

Questions like these sound absurd to people who haven't experienced sexual assault. *Of course it's not the victim's fault.* But for a long time, I couldn't escape these questions, either. They played on an endless loop in my head. I couldn't answer them, so I suppressed them as best I could.

After I was raped, I struggled to come to grips with what had happened. When the memories popped in my head, I felt physical pain in my chest, and shivers throughout my body. Only when the pain became too much to bear alone did I reach out for help.

I returned home from university and told my mum about the assault. The moment the words left my mouth, I crumbled. Months had passed, but it was the first time I'd spoken about the event out loud. I stopped suppressing the memory and my emotions, and they all came flooding out.

My mother did her best to help me, but unfortunately my pain was familiar to her, too. She shared her story with me; how she was also raped by someone she knew and trusted. She tried to seek justice. She brought the man to court. But she couldn't get a conviction. And so, she had to learn to heal and survive on her own.

Even after staying with my mother, I could not escape the feelings that were still inside of me. Eventually, I stopped talking to my mom about how I felt or what I needed because I couldn't safely process those conversations. I shut down. I sank into a hollow, desolate, dehumanized state.

I felt hopeless.

The world had shown me that no matter what I did, no matter what I wanted, no matter who I trusted and who I did not, I was not safe. Someone could take everything from me. All they had to do was decide that they wanted to.

The same thoughts churned repeatedly in my mind. I thought I was powerless, which meant I thought I was worthless. I thought that if another person *did* see some value in me, they could take it without a fight because I would not fight them…Because I did not fight him.

I decided that if men wanted my body, they could have it. But this time, I would give it freely. *You can't take it from me if I give it away.* Instead of facing my feelings, I projected self-confidence and self-control. At least…I tried.

What I wanted to do was sidestep my shame altogether. I tried to force feelings of self-empowerment by using my only feature that appeared to have any value—my body. I took to a few online forums and posted dozens of pictures of myself. My profiles filled up with pictures of me in bikinis, skin-tight dresses and miniskirts, and in some I was fully nude, but they were tasteful shots that didn't reveal any censorable parts of me. Through the guise of "influencing," I used my figure as a direct measurement for my self-worth. When the impressions came—the likes, shares, and reposts—I felt valuable. And when they didn't…well, that was a sign I needed to post more.

One day, as I was scrolling through a website peppered with random ads, I saw my own face staring back at me. It was a photo of my face, but someone superimposed it on another person's nude body. "HOT SINGLES IN YOUR AREA WANT TO MEET YOU" boasted the banner underneath the picture. I laughed at first—a misplaced emotion—then felt my shame crash into me like a tidal wave.

Even when I tried to take control of my own image, strangers online stole it from me. They took the only valuable thing about me and repurposed it for their own gain. I was never safe.

I'd thought I was on the path to self-improvement, but seeing my twisted image reflected back to me like that showed me how far I'd strayed. I'd been reduced to a "hot single" in someone's area by an online stranger. And if I was seeing this ad, then it was likely other people I knew were seeing it, too. My friends, my colleagues, maybe even my dad.

I left social media after that, but my body still found its way to the Internet in other ways. I sent scantily-clad photos of myself to a boy I dated, and when we broke up, he posted them online. And once they're online, they're online forever. Even today, I know they're still out there somewhere, waiting to be found by someone who connects them back to me. I've seen them.

Every once in a while, I'm still flushed with shame when I think about how much of my body is out there. I was especially terrified someone might find me online when I started my new career. I refused to make appearances on podcasts, give keynote speeches, or put my name in any programs for fear that a simple Google search would reveal my shame.

As I moved up in my career, I received more requests to publicize my work. Moving away from academia into the public sector meant exposing myself to the public eye. I started to show myself at events and conferences, but the more I did, the worse I felt. Every time my work posted a video of me, I refused to share the link on my own channel. I hid from my podcast appearances, my radio discussions, and my guest interviews. I lost sleep every night for weeks, for months, waiting for my past to expose me and send my whole world crashing down. The more I creeped toward the spotlight, the more I wanted to disappear.

The underlying shame from my sexual trauma continued to hamper my ability to function for years. I struggled to make any eye contact with my colleagues. I avoided answering the phone until the other person left a voicemail for why they'd called. I constantly monitored my website to see when people viewed it. Each time they did I was filled with anxiety. Every time I saw someone on my website, I thought, *They're going to know. Someone's going to out me. They'll find my pictures. They'll show my mistakes to the world.*

The more time passed, the more my shame held me back from what I wanted. I wanted a successful career. I wanted to be a speaker. I wanted to be an author. I wanted to be someone who could advise people—but I needed media attention to do those things. I needed name recognition and a personal brand. That terrified me. Every time I posted on Twitter, my stomach leapt up into my chest. *The more people see me, the more they can use my past against me.*

But no one actually wanted to hurt me—I was the only one punishing me for my past.

Finally, I grew exhausted with myself. I was tired of making myself sick with stress and shame. I thought, *This isn't healthy. I should be able to move on from the past and be successful. My past mistakes shouldn't hold back my future success. I'm purposely limiting myself. Enough is enough.*

I couldn't change what was out there. I couldn't change what happened to me. I still can't. The only thing I have control over is how my past affects the rest of my life. My mistakes, my past, they didn't force me to limit myself. They presented an opportunity for me to learn from them and grow.

Trauma Responses

Once we better understand why humans behave the way we do, we can take better control of our responses and reactions to trauma. We can be more forgiving to ourselves. We can heal.

Imagine waking up one morning in the body of a stranger. You look at your hands, wiggle your fingers, and the motions feel unfamiliar. When you get up and make your way to the mirror, you recognize your face, but it looks…different. Your eyes are the same shape, your nose is the same size, your lips are the same shade of pink, but there is a distance between the person in the mirror and the person looking into it. They feel miles away. They look empty inside.

As you study this reflection, you realize you're filthy. The dirt and grime don't appear in your reflection, but you feel it all over you. It's caked on your skin, layer after layer, and it feels heavy. You hop in the shower and scrub yourself until your arms and legs ache. The water runs clear but the filthy feeling doesn't leave. No amount of scrubbing makes it go away.

Throughout the day, nothing you do feels right. You fumble anything you hold. You feel the burning glares of everyone around you. Even walking from one place to another feels like you're carrying extra weight with you. Meanwhile, the dirt packs on thicker, though no one else can see it. Fear sets in. It doesn't seem like you'll ever escape this feeling.

This sensation of feeling like a stranger in your own skin is the devastating reality for many trauma victims, especially those who have suffered sexual assault. Crimes of a sexual nature are the most personal of crimes. They leave victims feeling as though their bodies were weaponized against them, imprisoning them while another person took control.

This response is uncomfortable but natural. Research into sexual assault victims has consistently revealed that victims feel a "dirtiness" or contamination following the assault. Many victims engage in behavioral coping strategies like compulsive washing.[8] This phenomenon is known as mental contamination (MC), which denotes "the feeling of internal dirtiness that arises without physical contact with contaminants."[9]

Unlike contact contamination, which can be traced back to a specific point of contact, mental contamination is difficult to locate and exists "inside the body" or "under the skin." Mental contamination can also appear after experiencing other forms of trauma, such as being flashed, being touched inappropriately outside of a sexual context, or observing sexual or violent acts.

One young woman I worked with told me about her mental contamination. "I feel…tainted," she said quietly, looking down at her raw hands. "I feel like I can't wash off the feeling of his hands on my skin."

Unsurprisingly, mental contamination and other side effects from trauma are often accompanied by self-directed emotions of disgust, shame, and revulsion. Through in-depth interviews with victims, peer-reviewed studies have demonstrated that feelings of internal dirtiness can be overwhelming and immune to external cleaning.

"Even after I showered, I felt that my friends could tell."

"Dirt can be washed away, but not this."

"It's like a dirty film on my skin that can't be removed."

"I am stuck with this forever."

Sometimes, trauma responses manifest through more abstract sensations. After my assault, I had an overwhelming urge to claw my way out of my own skin because the thought of it touching me felt like a violation. I couldn't handle the smallest physical contact with anyone. The moment a friend, a colleague, or even a family member embraced me in a hug, my skin burned like fire. The knowledge that the burning sensation was psychosomatic (not real) did nothing to soothe it.

I still struggle with physical contact today. It's something I anticipate I will struggle with for the rest of my life. The man I believed to be safe used my trust as a weapon, so I struggle to trust anyone else. It took me years to allow even my family to hug me. Even now, any time someone touches me, my body instinctively tightens. My pulse quickens. My breathing hitches. They may only want to show me affection, but I am filled with dread.

This is not to say these symptoms can't ever go away. Sometimes they do. Sometimes they soften without fading completely. There are coping mechanisms designed to help victims overcome the most egregious reminders of their trauma. We'll cover some of those mechanisms in Chapter 7.

For now, and quite possibly forever, I am still working through my own trauma. I am still finding new ways to feel shame for past mistakes. It would be dishonest and erroneous for me to state that this is a fast process. It's not. Healing is a continuous and effortful process, but it is a necessary journey to feel at home in your own body again.

The Only Way Out Is Through

No matter how valid our life choices are, the memories preceding traumatic experiences—and of the event itself—tend to induce feelings of shame. Feelings of regret, confusion, embarrassment, and betrayal are normal and can be frustrating to work through. Trauma distracts us from the healing process because we often can't help but replay the event on an endless loop, hoping to find where we went wrong.

In reality, the choices we make under traumatic stress have little to do with who we are at our core. They are our bodies' instinctual responses, designed to keep us safe and functional. Even when total safety isn't possible, these responses are still our best chance at survival. Our behaviors are worth examining, but they are not worth destroying our self-concept over.

We'll explore more about how trauma affects our choices in a later chapter, but for now it's worth stepping back and taking a deep breath. Facing shame often means facing some of the most difficult moments of our lives, and that's no small feat. Before we step forward to face our shame, let's acknowledge the effort we're about to make.

Everyone's healing journey is different, because the source of everyone's shame is different. The only part of the journey that remains the same is the confrontation. The only way to overcome the mountain of shame is to acknowledge it, examine it, and move through it. To become truly resilient and empowered, we must address shame head-on.

The first step on my healing journey was to discover the "why" behind my own actions, reactions, and feelings. I realized part of the reason I was hurting was because I was confused. I didn't understand why I didn't fight back against my attacker, or why I suddenly felt shame about my online presence when it once felt empowering. I didn't know myself anymore. I felt like a puzzle—I couldn't put the picture together because I didn't have all the pieces.

This realization started the learning journey that would eventually lead me to where I am today. I dove headfirst into the field of psychology, seeking answers to the questions that kept me up at night and kept me isolated. The more I learned, the more pieces of the puzzle I put in place.

Chapter 5

Finding Your Self

"You have power over your mind—not outside events.
Realize this, and you will find strength."
–Marcus Aurelius

Right after finishing my undergraduate degree, I received a scholarship to start my PhD studies. I was 21 years old and skipped the Masters' year that many of my new colleagues had under their belts. I felt miles behind everyone else in the program. My two new supervisors assured me the extra work I completed to earn my place was experience enough, but I was skeptical. Still, I was so excited to take on this new challenge. It was something I'd dreamed about for years.

I was still reeling from my traumatic experience when I enrolled in the PhD program. I hadn't yet rebuilt my self-concept and I wasn't convinced I could make it to graduation. At that point in my life, I'd gone through so many different versions of myself—

the shy bookworm, the social outcast, the party girl, the antisocial shut-in. I didn't know what my self-concept would look like during this next phase of life.

Before the term started, I spent the summer planning exactly how I would take on the world. Whatever happened next, I would make the most of it. I believed I owed it to myself and to others. Young women like me, from my background, with my experiences, didn't often get this sort of chance. And that's what it felt like to me—a chance, not something I'd earned.

I was thrilled when the first day finally came. My hard work was paying off, and I was motivated to keep up the good work. Then I attended my first official PhD meeting on campus and met with my supervisors in their office.

In this meeting, they explained what I would face over the next three and a half years. They walked me through the overall aims of a PhD and the common hurdles to expect. They outlined the level of expertise I needed to gain to earn my doctorate. And they reminded me that not everyone makes it through the program.

This was, of course, a standard introductory meeting. Every student attended one. The program's goal was to make sure students maintained realistic expectations of its requirements. But this meeting didn't feel standard to me. It felt personal. It seemed to me like these people were peering straight through my blazer and saw my self-concept…and they didn't like what they saw.

I was overwhelmed, and the feeling only grew worse as the meeting continued. With each new explanation of a task, I felt my arms grow heavier, until a part of me wondered how I would carry this weight out of the room. Self-doubt swelled inside me, causing me to wonder whether I could get through the program at all. Then a nasty thought crept up on me. It started as a whisper, then grew loud enough to drown out the voices of everyone else in the room: *You are making a mistake. You're not supposed to be here.*

I left the meeting as fast as I could. I walked straight past my office to the bus station. I wanted to go home and wallow in my own self-doubt. On the way, I did what I always did when I felt stressed, sad, or overwhelmed: I called my dad.

"Hello?"

The sound of his voice opened the floodgates inside of me. I burst into tears.

"I can't do this, Dad," I whimpered.

I told him about the meeting in as much detail as I could remember. I told him I didn't think I had what it would take—I didn't even understand how I got there in the first place. I wanted to quit before someone else in the program, or worse, someone else in the industry, realized I didn't deserve my place. I didn't deserve any of it.

Dad didn't stop me. He allowed me to get it all out, even as I spent the next five minutes repeatedly saying that the university made a big mistake allowing a fraud like me through their doors. When I was done and too exhausted to keep talking, he stayed silent for a second.

"You've got this, Ab—"

"No, Dad, you don't understand! I—" I started to cut him off, but he kept talking.

"I know you feel overwhelmed right now, but you can do this. You can do anything you put your mind to. Look what you have been through, look at what you have overcome already. This, this is nothing compared to what you have already done. So, dust yourself off, get back on your feet, and remember who you are."

It was like a switch flipped when I heard those words.

I've never been a confident person. I have always struggled to believe in myself. The only thing I've never struggled with is working hard. Somewhere inside me, I knew I could do this too, but that part of me was buried under stress, shame, and self-doubt. My dad's words forced me to self-reflect, and when I looked back, I saw how many times I tenaciously pursued the things I wanted. I was not someone who shied away from hard work. If anything, my work filled me with passion and helped push me through life.

In the moments after meeting my supervisors I forgot who I was, what I was capable of, and how normal it is to feel overwhelmed during a big life change.

"Thanks, Dad," I said softly.

"I know you can do this, Abbie. You know you can do this too. Think of everything you've already overcome. If you can get through all of that, you'll get through this."

He was right.

Being in the room with my supervisors felt like sinking underwater, unable to find the surface to catch my breath. I was overwhelmed because I was afraid of running out of air. But when I took a moment to relax, I could let the current guide me, watch the bubbles swirl around me, and see the sun poke through the surface. All I needed was a swift kick in the right direction to move forward. When I realized this, my fear of being a fraud dissipated.

Self-Concept: A Deep Dive

The most successful journeys are the ones where everyone involved understands the goals, the risks, and the expectations. When you set off on your journey toward empowerment, you must first understand what you're going to face along the way. With a better understanding of where shame comes from and why it's important, you are one step closer to reaching empowerment. The next leg of your journey involves knowing how your shame manifests for you, how it affects your self-concept, and how your self-concept helps you practice resilience.

The first obstacle to overcoming shame is figuring out what makes up your self-concept. Shame is a warning that you're acting against your sense of self. So, knowing who you are, who you want to be, and who you want to avoid becoming helps you recognize the root of any shame you feel. The stronger your self-concept, the better equipped you are to process shame in a healthy way. This can all sound abstract, though, so think of it this way.

The way your self-concept functions as a tether for your behavior is much like the tether freedivers use. I am fascinated by freedivers, people who choose to forgo an oxygen tank in favor of moving more freely during a deep-water dive. And the notion of exploring one's self-concept dozens of meters underwater with just a single rope back to the surface is the perfect analogy for the self-concept.

When experienced freedivers descend more than thirty meters below the surface of the water, they experience a sensation called freefall. Freefall happens after divers pass the point of neutral buoyancy. Before freefall the body wants to naturally rise back to the surface. After freefall, gravity overcomes buoyancy and divers start to sink.

Freedivers often compare freefalling to flying. At this depth, divers experience true floating, gliding through water with unparalleled freedom. They are less distracted by physical exertion, since the forces of nature take control. They are surrounded by serene silence, which leaves them room to focus on relaxation, self-reflection, and mindfulness.

There are unusual risks when divers enter freefall, though. Down in the open water, divers can become disoriented, losing sense of which way is up, down, or sideways. And if they can't navigate their way back to the surface, they will drown—remember, they have no oxygen tank. This is where the tether comes in.

The weighted tether freedivers use is their lifeline. No matter what choices they make or how far they freefall, they can always find their way back to the surface with the tether. So, as long as they can hold their breath and locate the tether, they are safe.

The strength of our self-concept is our tether for daily life. As long as we can locate it, we can find our way back to who we are. This gives us the freedom to live life without the fear of overwhelming shame. We can still expect to experience some shame, but when we do, we can return to our self-concept and remind ourselves of who we are.

As mentioned in Chapter 2, there is still plenty of scientific discourse surrounding The Self. The self-reflective process to determine who you are is difficult, even outside of the context of trauma, stress, or duress. It's even harder to return the safety of your self-concept if you don't know where to find it.

Losing your self-concept doesn't always occur after experiencing trauma—it is sometimes a gradual occurrence that takes place over weeks, months, or years. It can come from a draining relationship, career, or an otherwise routine event. It can also occur after an illness or a sudden loss. There are many ways a person can drift away from their self-concept without their noticing.

When your emotions and behaviors drift too far from your self-concept, you may notice yourself developing new patterns of behavior that don't line up with your old self. This shift can be positive or negative. A positive shift may actually strengthen your self-concept, making you feel more mature, appreciative, grateful, and responsible. But a negative shift can bring about feelings of bitterness, loneliness, frustration, and irritability.

After my sexual assault, I felt like someone ripped away my self-concept and left me in freefall. I felt alone, drifting toward the ocean floor with no hope of resurfacing. I was angry at the world for letting it happen to me. I was angry at other people for knowing who they were, for keeping track of their tethers. I was angry at myself because I failed to stay safe. It didn't feel fair.

Before I could make it back to safety, I needed a new tether. Without the safety and comfort of my old self-concept, I had no choice but to build my sense of self back up from nothing. I didn't know where to start, but I knew I couldn't move forward without figuring it out.

Finding Your Self-Concept: Where to Begin?

Re-locating your self-concept is hard, but I like to think about it like running an experiment, except you're both the subject and the examiner. You move through your day like always, making choices that feel right in the moment, and letting yourself experience whatever emotions arise. Then, at the end of the day, you reflect on and observe your choices to try to find what traits they have in common. *Do these choices mean I'm kind? Am I selfish? Am I hardworking? Do I feel good about my actions?*

However, there's a reason we don't conduct experiments on ourselves in the scientific community: the subject's awareness of the experiment can change the results. Knowing you're searching for your true Self is enough information to influence your decisions. You may overthink choices. You may place too much weight on some behaviors and not enough on others. You may not understand which behaviors are affected by shame or trauma, and that confusion is enough to change the shape of your self-concept.

The tricky thing about finding your self-concept is that you can't always tell which traits are temporary and which are permanent. There's a difference between feeling happy and being a happy person. There's a difference between feeling confident with a new outfit or haircut and being a confident person. How do you determine which traits are a part of that central Self?

When I began to pick up the pieces of myself, I didn't know which of my behaviors were influenced by my trauma and shame, and which were true signs of who I was at my core. For example, my self-worth felt like it hinged on how valuable others found my body. As long as others admired me, lusted after me, and desired me, I felt valuable. And I was so desperate to prove I wasn't worthless that I devalued myself.

I placed too much of my self-worth in how I looked. It makes sense in hindsight—my physical appearance was what pulled me out of solitude in primary school. The way I looked made it easier to convince people to give me what I wanted, whether it was drugs, sex, or any other distraction from my pain. My looks helped me fill a void in my life, so they became the most important part of my self-concept.

Moving forward, I used that information to inform my new self-concept. I didn't want to place so much stock in my looks. Before building up a strong self-concept, you must recognize what may be influencing your choices and behaviors. That's how you separate the permanent traits from the temporary ones. As you identify the biological, psychological, and sociological mechanisms working outside of your conscious mind, you'll begin to see a clearer picture of who you are at your core.

Self-Concept Through Change

Even as you zero in on your true Self, changing circumstances can still introduce a level of uncertainty around your self-concept. Big life changes like a new job, a new boyfriend, a big move, a growing family, exam week at school…they all cause stress. Stress from change often leads to shameful behaviors, which ultimately threaten how we see ourselves.

When we're stressed out from change, we're more likely to lash out at others. We might make decisions that only help relieve the stress in the short-term, like drinking, smoking, or binging on comfort foods. We skip the gym, throw off our sleep schedule, avoid completing tasks because we are too busy worrying about them needing to be done. We swear we'll fix these problems when the stress is gone or when life settles down again. But the more we engage in poor behaviors, the further we move away from our ideal self.

The goal is to make decisions that make us feel better about who we are. This can look like choosing carrots over cake, a novel over network news, or a cat nap over a nightclub. Sometimes, it can look like the opposite. The outcome doesn't matter as long as your decisions feel true to you. The better we feel about who we are, the more likely we are to show resilience in the face of change, instead of crumbling beneath it.

Human beings are comfort seekers. We like what feels familiar, what feels predictable, because it makes us feel safe. When we act in predictable ways, we are certain of the outcome based on previous experience. We like to avoid risk when possible. Familiarity is safe. It's change that is risky.

Avoiding change makes perfect sense from an evolutionary perspective. Erring on the side of caution is how early humans avoided some of the many dangers they faced. There is evidence that our inclination to avoid uncertainty has been passed down through our genes. We still see its biological markers when we experience uncertainty today. We look both ways before crossing the street, we sniff the milk before drinking it, and we set multiple alarms to wake up on a big day. Better safe than sorry, right?

Humans are hard-wired to avoid uncertainty and react negatively to change. The stress response (commonly known as the fight or flight response) is the default response to uncertainty, which is reflected physiologically in high vagally mediated heart rate variability. Don't worry if you don't know what that means, we'll cover this response in depth in the next chapter. For now, all you need to know is that when we deploy the stress response, we have a hard time regulating our emotions.

Stress from times of change manifests differently for different people. While the stress response is our default, some people can inhibit this reaction through psychological factors that increase their perception of safety. Some people view their body's stress response as a rush, which motivates them to work harder and succeed. They see stressful challenges and times of change as a way to prove their grit.

For others, the stress response intensifies the fear of uncertainty. They ruminate on their fear and search for ways to make it go away. This reaction is often accompanied by feelings of anxiety, negative self-talk, and reduced self-care. People who fear uncertainty spend their time trying to prepare for every possible scenario. They stop being present for everyday life and end up trapped in a cycle of asking, "*What if this happens?*" until they burn out.

Change is uncomfortable, but that doesn't mean we stop adapting to it. We don't want to retreat back to a clearer, more familiar version of ourselves for the sake of comfort. Change can make us feel different from those around us, and feeling like we don't fit in creates stress on a biological level. However, change is also a necessary part of growing, recovering, and living a healthy life.

The Main Self-Concept Components

To find or build a new self-concept to tether yourself, even through times of change, stress, and trauma, research identifies three traits worth strengthening.[10] Positive self-esteem, self-efficacy, and perceived locus of control are the traits that contribute to our sense of resilience. When these traits are strong, they provide a clearer picture of our self-concepts and help us stay true to ourselves under pressure.

Self-esteem refers to how we value and perceive ourselves. If our beliefs about ourselves are generally positive, we are more likely to believe we can adapt to challenging environments. Positive self-esteem makes us feel more comfortable taking calculated risks, thus reducing the fear of uncertainty that often comes with change. Self-esteem is a major factor in resilience and self-empowerment as well, and we'll cover how a bit later.

Self-efficacy refers to how capable we feel when it comes to achieving goals. When we believe we're good at making choices that help us succeed, our sense of self-efficacy grows. For example, most of us know we're physically capable of going to the gym, but not all of us believe we'll actually stick to a new gym routine. Self-efficacy can be considered as the way we feel about our willpower. If we believe we have strong willpower, we're more likely to suck it up and go to the gym regularly. If we believe our willpower is weak, we probably won't even try on those new workout shorts.

Finally, psychologists consider **perceived locus of control** a major factor in our behavior and self-concept. Our locus of control refers to our perception about how much control we have over our own lives. Put simply, this concept wants to know: do you believe your destiny is controlled by you, or by external forces?

People with an **internal locus of control** believe they are ultimately responsible for what happens in their lives. If they fail a test, it's because they didn't study hard enough. Empirical research has shown that individuals with an internal locus of control adapt to change better. [11,12]They're more likely to show behavioral commitment to change instead of slipping back into old habits or routines.

People with an **external locus of control** believe their lives are determined mostly by outside forces. If they fail a test, they believe it's because the test was too hard, the teacher graded unfairly, or the testing room was too stuffy. Individuals with an external locus of control are less likely to show strong critical thinking skills, which are crucial for adapting to change.

A person's locus of control plays a large part in their self-concept, especially when it comes to overcoming self-doubt, raising self-esteem, and improving self-efficacy. Recognizing accomplishments as a direct result of an individual's hard work is vital for overcoming self-doubt. Individuals with an external locus of control are more likely to assign the success to an outside force, like a lucky break or a miracle, instead of their own capabilities. On the other hand, individuals with an internal locus of control are more likely to contribute their success to themselves, which helps raise their self-esteem.

The beauty of the human species lies in the unique complexity of each person's experience. As we grow up and live through new experiences, our Self shifts. New relationships, careers, personal growth, belief systems, traumatic experiences, sudden loss, and everything else life has to offer us change who we are. We make gradual changes until old versions of ourselves are unrecognizable. The more we experience, the more we grow.

Our capacity for growth may be beautiful in the abstract, but it does nothing to stop times of change from causing feelings of loneliness, stress, or confusion. Periods of change usually coincide with mental health struggles, feelings of isolation and anxiety, and a general sense of exhaustion. We might even experience moments of regret. These moments can trigger shame despite our species' natural inclination to use new experiences to grow.

Imposter Syndrome: Self-Concept Meets Self-Doubt

Everyone has their own moments of freefall: times when we feel out of our depths even in familiar situations. I have yet to come across a high achieving professional who hasn't had moments of self-doubt about their work. When this self-doubt appears, we tend to react as if we're the only person in the room who feels it; everyone else is supposed to be here, but not us.

This is imposter syndrome: the feeling that we don't deserve the success we have, the position we're in, or the opportunities presented to us. It feels like some divine accident or lucky streak brought us here, and it's only a matter of time before someone more worthy catches on. Imposter syndrome makes our success feel like a shameful secret. This feeling is especially common during times of change, like at a new job, in a new relationship, or any time you join a new community. It's a vicious manifestation of the fear you don't belong.

When I left my meeting with my supervisors, my self-doubt took control of me. I felt moments away from a full-on, Scooby-Doo-esque unmasking, where one of my colleagues would chase me from the bus stop, rip off my mask, and say, "Ah ha! See? She's a fraud!"

Imposter syndrome is one of the side-effects of a self-concept that isn't strong enough to withstand periods of change or stress. Imposter syndrome affects all three of the main components of a strong self-concept. Imposter syndrome can take down people with internal or external loci of control. Even if you typically have an internal locus of control, imposter syndrome can still catch up to you. It can make you feel like you made a series of bad decisions that ultimately led you to the wrong place. Feeling like a fraud takes a toll on your self-efficacy by convincing you that every success is a fluke, not a well-earned result of hard work.

The occasional sense of imposter syndrome is normal. Being scared of failure means you care about what you're doing and want to do it well. When you start a new career, you can never know what to fully expect. You'll have to spend time learning new skills, meeting new colleagues, and learning the lay of the land. If you want to excel at a new opportunity, you will have to work through this period of uncertainty. Additionally, even within the same organization, you may be thrust into situations and roles that are new to you.

Imposter syndrome is more common in the workplace than anywhere else. In fact, regardless of the career or position in a hierarchy, an estimated 70 percent of people experience these feelings.[13] When you feel like an imposter, you're scared that at any moment, you'll be 'found out' by those around you. You expect someone to realize you're just as incapable as you feel inside, and once they know, they'll take it all away from you.

The problems with imposter syndrome begin when the period of change ends, but the feelings of inadequacy do not. Research has also shown that the impacts of a prolonged sense of imposter syndrome can be debilitating.[14] It can lead to social isolation and mental health issues, such as depression and severe anxiety.

Feelings of inadequacy are exhausting. Fearing uncertainty is exhausting. Constantly reassessing whether you have what it takes to make it through life is a quick way to burn yourself out. Once you understand your self-concept, you can address these fears and feelings. Fear of the unknown may be a biological predisposition, but so is our best chance at allaying those fears—the practice of self-reflection.

For me, my imposter syndrome was my brain reminding me of the person I used to be. As I sat in classrooms filled with young professionals, I kept thinking, *If only you knew. If only they knew. I'm not supposed to be here.* I thought that if my colleagues found out about my past, they'd finally see the side of myself I couldn't escape: the version of me who wasn't fit to become a doctor of anything.

Self-Reflection

It took some self-reflection to realize my brain wasn't trying to sabotage me—it was trying to remind me how far I'd come, so I was less likely to backslide under stress. The shame I felt about my old self was healthy because it motivated me to keep moving away from her. I wanted nothing more than to succeed in this program. The stakes were some of the highest I'd ever experienced. I couldn't afford to take a night off at the bottom of a bottle anymore. This was the real deal.

In a way, the fear I felt was actually beneficial for rebuilding my self-concept. I was afraid of failing, which meant some part of me knew I could succeed. I was afraid of falling back into old habits, which means this version of myself wanted to move past them. The more I learned about my new self-concept, the less I wanted to revisit the old ones. While I continued to grieve the person I used to be, I felt the first shred of hope about the person I could become.

Chapter 6
Facing Shame

*"A moral being is one who is capable of reflecting
on his past actions and their motives—approving
of some and disapproving of others."*
–Charles Darwin

When I told my parents I wanted to go for my PhD, they had polar opposite reactions. My dad was thrilled.

"You've got this," he said. "You can do anything you put your mind to."

My mum, though…wasn't so supportive.

Both reactions were unsurprising to me. While my dad always tried to support any healthy ambition I had, my mum was quick to dismiss any growth opportunity I took on. When I broke from my partying days to focus on school, she called me a bore. When I stopped sleeping around, she called me a prude. When I dove back into my schoolwork to make up for lost time, she called me a nerd.

Sometimes, when my shame creeps in, it whispers to me in my mother's voice.

Years before I considered earning my PhD, before I thought about becoming Doctor Abbie, I was stuck in another version of my self-concept: a version of myself who was more interested in drinking, taking drugs, and ignoring schoolwork. In fact, when I was seventeen, I failed out of college.

In the UK, our school system is split up differently than in the US. Primary school is grades 1-7, secondary school is grades 8-11, and instead of a single, senior year, we have college, or A levels. And I couldn't attend University without an A level certificate.

The deepest parts of my shame spiral occurred in my first year of A levels, and I flunked out of most of my classes. My psychology class was one of the classes I failed. The psychology teacher, Ms. Moon, hated me. I was disruptive, uninterested, and was a reputable troublemaker. If I wanted to graduate and move on to University, I had to convince her to let me back in her class for a second chance.

I approached her office after classes one day. I knocked softly on the door, silently hoping she wasn't in.

"Ms. Moon?" I called quietly.

"Yes, come in," I heard her say. I took a deep breath and opened the door.

Ms. Moon was a short, curvy, middle-aged woman. Her thick glasses framed her kind eyes, and her wavy hair draped around her freckled face. She looked up from her desk and seemed surprised to see me. I'm sure I was a sight—no longer puffed up with false empowerment, I felt smaller than the last time I'd seen her. Instead of indignant, I was humble.

"I want to do better," I said. "I really want this."

Ms. Moon said nothing for a moment. She looked me up and down, measuring how much I meant it. The corners of her mouth started to slip into a frown.

"If you let me come back, I'll put the work in, I promise," I stammered. "How about if I write you one essay a week? I'll do it every week until the end of the term. I just need a little bit of support."

Her expression softened at that. She felt how much I wanted to redeem myself.

"Okay, Abbie," she said, "let's give it a try."

Ms. Moon's acceptance motivated me to make similar deals with my former Literature and Graphic Design teachers, too. The extra work would prove difficult, but it was also a welcome distraction from my old coping mechanisms. I didn't have the time to fall back in with my old friends or unhealthy habits. I had to throw myself into my schoolwork or risk failing again.

The year was hard. There was no Hollywood montage of me studying hard and acing my first papers. The first few weeks, I received D's on almost every assignment. But I got into a flow, and those D's turned into C's, then B's. I had a solid goal to reach, and I was motivated to prove myself.

Some days, Ms. Moon would read a student's essay aloud to help her class better grasp what she looked for in an A-grade paper. She usually read from the same five students' essays, which was unsurprising to the rest of us. But one day, she told the class she'd be reading mine.

A laugh rose up from the back of the room. A boy turned to his friend and whispered, "I'd rather die than take notes on anything she wrote."

Ms. Moon heard him, but instead of calling attention to his remark, she moved to me and sat down in the empty seat beside me.

I looked up, confused, and she gave me a small wink. She cleared her throat and began to read from my paper. She usually stuck to a paragraph or two, but she read out the entire essay. As she read, she interrupted herself to loudly point out what I did well.

When she finished, she smiled at me and returned my work. At the top, a large, red "A" decorated the first page.

"Well done," she whispered, and returned to the front of the room.

I spent a lot of time with Ms. Moon that year. Without a friend group to join, Ms. Moon invited me to share lunch in her classroom each day. We talked psychology together over sandwiches and apple slices. I often stayed after class to finish up my extra work in her room. She grew from a teacher to a dear friend to a second, more supportive maternal figure.

The more I applied myself, the more I succeeded in my courses, and the better I felt about myself. My self-efficacy and self-esteem grew every time I submitted an extra credit assignment. This time around, I realized I loved psychology as a subject. Not only did I love it, I was good at it.

I believe that psychology and Ms. Moon saved me. My love for the subject became an outlet for all of my extra energy. I found a way to throw myself into something without dangerous consequences. My newfound enthusiasm spread to my other courses, too. I stopped viewing my education as an annoyance and saw it for what it was: a way to grow and achieve goals.

A few years later when I experienced sexual trauma, lost my self-concept, and was at risk of losing everything I'd worked for, psychology saved me again. I remembered how much of my emotional experience came from underlying mechanisms working outside of my conscious control. At the worst period of my life, I fell back on psychology to help me heal and grow.

Here is what I recalled: shame is a natural human reaction to behavior, not an indication that we are less than or unworthy. To separate shameful experiences from our self-concept, we must understand the driving forces of our actions: the biological, psychological, and sociological underpinnings of human behavior. Facing shame means separating our emotions from our self-concept. Once we understand that what we do isn't always indicative of who we are, we're closer to reaching true empowerment.

Once we've got a clear picture of our self-concept, the next step to facing shame is sorting through our emotional experiences. We're looking for what experiences signal a need for change, and which are natural parts of being a human. We can do this by examining the experiences through a strong knowledge of our behavioral roots and patterns.

The Real Pain Behind Shame

A basic understanding of my body and mind armed me with the knowledge I needed to face my shame. Day by day, I learned to control how I felt. On days when I felt low, I forced myself to go to the gym and work out. I knew the endorphins my body released would reduce my perception of pain, both physically and emotionally.

A lot of my shame came from my loneliness, my longing to be loved and the fear I was unlovable. I wanted so badly to appear strong and independent, like someone who didn't care what others thought of her, but deep down I knew how much I craved someone who cared.

I was ashamed of how sharp loneliness felt, but I reminded myself that humans are built to care deeply for our social relationships. Indeed, psychologists have discovered that within the human brain, the neural pathways used to process physical pain are the same ones used for processing social pain. This overlap in our neural circuitry means that social pain literally hurts us, like a scraped knee or a broken bone.

There is proof of this in the way we speak about pain: most people are familiar with phrases like "My heart was broken" or "It felt like a gut-punch." We might say we feel like we can't breathe or that we've been kicked in the stomach after a breakup. In almost every culture, there is a presence of expressions that combine physical and emotional pain to describe experiences. However, until recently, there was still debate around whether this overlap was more than a convenient metaphor.

In 2011, researchers aimed to put this debate to rest. They set out to demonstrate the overlap between social and physical pain. Their experiment gave new meaning to the idea that rejection "hurts" by mapping the similarities between their subjects' responses to painful social memories and physical pain.

It's difficult to set up a study wherein the participants must experience pain. For one thing, it's tricky to convince any group of people to sign up for a painful experience. Throw in the caveat that you can't reveal the details of the experiment, and you're going to have an even harder time collecting a sample size. These researchers posted flyers around the streets of Manhattan, the marketplace on Facebook, and the ads on Craigslist. They promised $175 for anyone willing to talk about their most recent, ugly breakup while researchers scanned their brains. Forty people agreed to give it a shot.

Participants were hooked up to fMRI machines, then given two painful stimuli: one physical, one social. For the physical pain, participants received a hot poke on their arm (ranked from 2-8 on a pain scale.) For the social pain, they were asked to look at a picture of their ex with a cue-phrase directing them to focus on a specific experience the two shared together written underneath. After receiving the stimulus for each event, the participants rated how much they were affected, physically or mentally.

When the participants experienced the social pain, the areas of their brains responsible for processing the aversive component of physical pain (secondary somatosensory cortex; dorsal posterior insula) were activated. These findings revealed that social rejection and physical pain are not only similar in that they're both distressing—they also share a common representation in brain system responses.

The researchers went one step further and collated findings from over 500 previously published studies. Their goal was to demonstrate that activation in these brain regions is highly indicative of physical pain. This doesn't mean we experience a rejection from a partner the exact same as a stubbed toe, but the two sensations are meaningfully similar. The pain we feel from emotional experiences—like rejection, self-doubt, and even shame—is not in our imaginations.

This discovery suggests that treating social pain similar to physical pain is a valid method for reducing the hurt. So, when I say going to the gym helps me heal and makes me feel stronger, I'm referring to both my body and my mind. My endorphins muffle the deafening voices in my mind telling me I'm not good enough, not smart enough, or not capable enough to succeed. Even if I'm not feeling motivated to go work out, my knowledge of a workout's benefits helps me get up out of bed and make the effort anyway.

However, not every wound is cured by a Band-Aid, and not every painful feeling is cured by a quick jog. There are other underlying processes within the human brain that work in tandem to create unique, complex emotional experiences. This is one of many methods that, when used together, help us face and ultimately overcome shame.

Fight, Flight, or Freeze

In previous chapters we touched on the stress response humans experience when they feel threatened. Since our neural networks register multiple forms of pain, they also respond to multiple forms of threats. The threat of embarrassment can trigger our fight or flight response. The threat of rejection can do the same. Traumatic experiences set off our stress response whether they threaten physical or emotional consequences.

So, what happens in the brain when this response is triggered?

Our memories are designed to pay special attention when we're exposed to a threat: we call this process memory consolidation.[15] If an event is a threat to us, it is advantageous for us to remember that event as bad—we touch the hot stove once on purpose, then we never do it again. During a threat event, our stress response system springs into action, releasing corresponding stress hormones that tell the brain: "Hey, this experience has survival utility, and you need to remember this event because it's a threat to your safety." Then the brain responds, "Fantastic, thank you, I'll make a note of that. We'll remember that pain so vividly, we'll never want to touch a stove again."

But what if you want to forget the threatening event?

Trauma, by definition, comes from a shocking, scary, or dangerous event. For an event to be considered traumatic it must exceed the standard parameters of what we are emotionally equipped to deal with. Because of this adaptation, I replayed the memory of my own muffled crying for months. My brain didn't want to experience the trauma again, so it refused to let me forget it.

Although I would have given anything to forget my trauma, it's exactly what my threat detection system wants me to remember. So that memory will stay with me, and not only will it resurface periodically in my mind, it will also trigger a full nervous system response whenever it appears. My body enters a state of defense any time I'm confronted with that experience again. In other words, my trauma haunts me. My memories become the skeletons in my closet, and I am the monster under my own bed.

This process is more widely recognized as the "fight or flight" response. The phrase "fight or flight," coined by American physiologist Walter B. Cannon, is known by both scientists and laypeople. It's well established that all human beings have been equipped, through millions of years of evolution, with a fight (action) or flight (escape) instinct to increase their chances of survival when facing potential danger. In other words, during a threatening situation, humans will instinctively respond by either preparing to fight back and resist, or to run away.

It is less known, however, that there is a third potential response to threatening situations: the freeze response. Sometimes, in the face of danger, our bodies may become immobile. The instinct to freeze overwhelms all other possible responses.

Decades of research has shown that this freeze response may have served an important purpose in our evolutionary history.[16] For example, during an attack from a predator, where there is little chance of escaping or winning a fight, freezing or "playing dead" may have increased the chances of an animal's survival. Some predators released prey if they believed it to be dead already. This freeze response has since been demonstrated across several different species, as well as evidenced in humans during both field and laboratory experiments. Thus, freezing in the face of danger is not a sign of weakness or evidence of consent, it is a predetermined survival mechanism that is sometimes exercised to maximize the chance of survival.

In cases of sexual assault, there isn't always a clear escape route, nor is there always the possibility to fight to freedom. The victim's body defaults to the freeze response as a last-ditch effort to end the attack. In fact, it has been shown that anywhere from 12-50 percent of victims lay motionless and do not attempt to fight or escape the attacker during the attack.[17]

If what I've just said resonates with you, please know that you are not alone, and you are also not responsible for what happened to you.

This information was a crucial part of my healing journey following my attack. I found comfort in the knowledge that I wasn't consciously responsible for my reaction. I didn't choose to stay still and accept the violation. There wasn't a silent part of me somewhere deep inside that consented. While I healed, I told myself then, and still tell myself now: *just because it happened does not mean I allowed it to happen.*

While the knowledge brought me comfort, it did not prevent the pain. My understanding of the psychological processes happening in my mind did not stop them from happening. I couldn't prevent my brain from enacting dozens of safety measures to protect me. I still fell into a deep hole of sadness and regret. I still engaged in behaviors that caused me to feel even more shame. I still felt the searing pain of self-loss.

Traumatic Loss

Losing yourself after trauma can force a total transformation of your perception. Thoughts, spaces, and even people you once considered safe no longer give you comfort. Your own body can feel like a prison. When you look around after experiencing trauma, it can feel like the whole world is a little bit darker. This leaves people confused about where they stand, how they feel, and who they are in this new phase of life post-trauma.

The loss of identity goes far deeper than simply being confused or feeling out of place. Trauma can trigger a neurological rewiring in our brains. It is driven by a biological drive to escape the pain of trauma, so much so that the neural processes associated with a sense of self in the brain are vastly interrupted and even completely halted. It's no wonder trauma alters our normal behaviors and thought processes.

The experience of trauma, particularly trauma in early life while the brain is creating many pathways for the first time, can often lead to the development of Post-Traumatic Stress Disorder (PTSD). We see this often in victims of abuse. Considering the intense memory consolidation our brains impose during stressful events, it's no wonder so many survivors suffer from PTSD.

So, what do we do when we become our own worst nightmare? How do we prevent our memories from making us the monsters under our own beds?

When someone in our lives causes us pain, we sever the connection—the same solution applies to our own trauma. When our brains determine a traumatic experience is too painful to process, we experience suppression, which in turn triggers an emotional shutdown.

This shutdown reduces activation in the medial prefrontal cortex (MPFC), the anterior cingulate, the parietal cortex, and the insula. In some cases, the activity is completely muted. Collectively, these regions play a key role in memory (retrieval and consolidation) particularly in processing fear memory. They're also responsible for decision making, sensory perception, and creating and maintaining our self-concept.[18] As long as we're stuck in emotional suspension, we're in no position to grow.

In the book, *The Body Keeps the Score*, author Bessel Van Der Kolk reports of a study: "In response to the trauma itself, and in coping with the dread that persisted long afterward, these patients had learned to shut down the brain areas that transmit the visceral feelings and emotions that accompany and define terror. Yet in everyday life, those same brain areas are responsible for registering the entire range of emotions and sensations that form the foundation of our self-awareness, our sense of who we are."

If you look back at behaviors you engaged in while recovering from trauma, maybe even the behaviors you are currently engaging in, I hope this brings you a new level of understanding as to why you did not feel like you. If looking back at yourself brings you shame, remind yourself of this: it was not weakness that drove you, but a biological adaptation towards survival—an adaptation so strong that it changes your brain. Remind yourself that your drive to survive is not a shameful response. Once you acknowledge this, you can begin to rediscover your self-concept as it relates to your new phase of life.

Deathless Grief

Losing your self-concept can be as painful as losing a loved one. It may not sound as serious—after all, your self-concept isn't lost forever, nor is it a literal death—but the body experiences the same grief for ourselves as we feel for others. Psychologists refer to this process as "deathless grief."

When I started my journey to overcome shame and reach empowerment, I experienced self-grief. I first felt angry. I had moments of denial where I dismissed my pain and tried to squeeze myself back into my old self. I was depressed. I felt every stage of grief, sometimes all at once. And I deserved to grieve, as everyone does. A piece of me was gone, and I would never get it back.

Self-grieving isn't a common concept in public understanding, but it's a concept many people experience. When people grieve themselves, they often can't place why they feel the way they do. Most feel a sense of shame—like they don't have the right to be in a state of grief. I've spoken to plenty of people who resonated with the feeling but were unaware it had roots in psychology. It can be validating to discover that the emotional experience is backed by science.

Self-grief is complex. It's an in-between stage for people trying to understand who they are outside of who they've been. Skipping the self-grief stage is like trying to start a new relationship right after a devastating breakup. You can try to get to know yourself again, but the process will be tainted until you process your grief.

Some people are invigorated by the idea of starting over. It can be comforting to consider leaving behind all the bad we've experienced in favor of a clean slate. It gives us a chance to grow without the messy process of answering tough, introspective questions. So why do humans feel the need to grieve their former selves?

Humans aren't built for full metamorphosis. Our brains are gloriously plastic, meaning they are constantly shaped and reshaped by our experiences. We have an extraordinary ability to re-learn and discover new ideas throughout our lives. Even into adulthood, our brains continue to create new neural pathways that allow us to adapt to future experiences.

However, there are limits to this plasticity. We can form new paths, but we can never truly remove the old ones. It is impossible to fully restructure who we are. We can't shed our old self-concepts like shakes shed their skin and move forward unphased. Thus, to assume we can leave our past selves behind and start fresh is not realistic, nor is it conducive to healthy coping. We're not designed to start fresh simply because we decide we want to. We are the products of our past, both individually and collectively as a species.

This reality causes grief. There are memories we'd like to forget and lessons we'd like to unlearn. Facing trauma, shame, and periods of change cause a discomfort that leaves us yearning for the safety of stasis. But just as the butterfly cannot curl back up in its cocoon, we cannot regress into an old version of ourselves. The only way out is through. We have to move forward.

Moving through self-grief is not about starting fresh, but learning how our new self-concept integrates with our old self. This healing process involves not only reconstructing our internal self-concept, but also our social self-concept (how we perceive ourselves in relation to others). If we want to experience positive long-term adjustment, we must be realistic and try to strike a balance between identity maintenance of our past and future.

If you find yourself in self-denial, engaging in maladaptive coping mechanisms that lead you further down the wrong path, that doesn't mean you are past the point of no return. I lost count of the number of times I tried to cope by creating versions of myself that felt good, but did not truly reflect me. I did anything I could to recover what I lost, so much so that each time I tried to revisit my old self-concept, I ended up leaving behind a trail of shame and regret. I was only able to truly move forward when I sat down and asked myself the question: *Who am I now?*

Taking Back Your Self

I can't actually pinpoint a moment when I suddenly recognized my self-concept again. It was the result of an accumulation of my new behaviors—tough decisions, moments of introspection, setbacks and steps forward. I slowly gained the power to choose how I defined myself despite what I'd been through, not in spite of it. I learned enough self-awareness to think, *I have survived. I lost parts of myself along the way, but that's okay. I am not bulletproof, but I am strong enough to persevere. I'm a work in progress—any progress is good.*

Now, this is easier said than done, especially when your brain stops you from reconciling with your self-concept. If your neurological processes are stuck in emergency shutdown mode, your journey to regain your sense of self starts with firing up those brain regions. How do you manage this? Introspection.

The conscious act of introspection, most commonly defined as the act of purposefully examining one's own thoughts and feelings, strengthens the MPFC. Introspection is an effort toward recovery, which encourages the brain regions responsible for self-understanding to open back up. Clinical neuroscientists agree the practice of introspection is the hallmark of personal growth. When we introspect, we make progress toward healing from trauma, shame, and other painful experiences. It helps us develop a stronger self-concept, which brings us closer to empowerment.

Introspection is easier to practice with an established self-concept, but what if you're introspecting to find your self-concept in the first place? How can you trust your self-reflection if you don't yet trust yourself? The answer may seem simple, but it's true: start by giving yourself a break.

No one heals from their past overnight. The journey through shame to empowerment is filled with setbacks, relapses, and mistakes. You may try to force a version of your self-concept before realizing it's not a good fit. You'll keep making decisions that bring you shame. The end goal is not to eliminate shame, settle on a static self-concept, or become a self-loving guru.

When I restarted my second year of A levels, I wanted to quit a dozen times. The work was hard. The hours I spent studying dragged on longer than I thought was possible. Every "D" grade stung like fire. My self-concept was still fragile, and every setback felt like a reminder of my potential to fail. If I hadn't forgiven the little mistakes, I wouldn't have made it to the big wins. If I'd been too hard on myself, I wouldn't have made it.

During a growth period, the stakes feel insurmountably high. It feels like if you fail, you're letting yourself down, but you're also letting down everyone who cares about you. Your new boss is counting on you to succeed after a promotion. Your partner needs you to be healthy for them to be healthy. Your friends, your family, your community is relying on you to keep it together. The more you think about who you're failing, the more impossible success feels.

It's all too easy to feel shame about your behaviors when it feels like the world is relying on you to succeed by any means necessary. Expectations like this make a slip-up during a speech feel like the end of your career. They make it feel like forgetting to take the chicken out of the freezer means the family will starve because of your mistake.

Give yourself a break. Laugh it off (especially if you're a Brit, like me) and order some takeout. I promise you: no one else is as worried about your mistakes as you are.

Humans have a tendency to overestimate how much others care about our successes and failures. This concept is known as the overblown implications effect. We spend every moment of our lives inside our own heads, ruminating on our own choices. Our inner voice is the one we hear above all others. We're biased to believing everyone else thinks about our choices as much as we do, since our thoughts feel the most intense.

Research has shown that when we make a mistake, we often ruminate on how it felt and how other people will judge our behavior. In reality, observers care very little about it, and once it's over it's rarely considered again. You may think about how you accidentally misspelled your boss's name over email, or accidentally named the wrong author when publicly recalling a quote, but after listeners are exposed to it, maybe after a slight chuckle, they get on with their day. They don't give it another thought, but you? You're your own worst critic, and your faux pas fills you with shame. You're your own worst critic.

I've lost count of the number of times I've made a mistake while speaking on a podcast or in an interview. Each time after the words leave my lips, I feel my insides curl up into a ball of embarrassment! I still to this day feel the urge to shudder when I think of some mistakes, even if the mistake was nothing more than a mispronunciation.

We all get like this to some extent; the overblown implications effect is a side effect of being such a social species. It's not the feeling that matters—what matters is how we navigate through the feeling. If we're going to recover from a mistake, we can't dwell on how heavily it affects others. If our actions hurt someone, we apologize and make it right. Otherwise, we just need to go easy on ourselves!

The funny thing about the overblown implications effect is that it's a common experience for everyone. When you see someone else trip on a stair, stutter when speaking, or deliver a dead joke, they're likely to think you're going to remember it forever, too. But you probably won't remember it five minutes from when it happened. We can't all spend our time thinking about everyone else's mistakes. There's not enough time in a day.

When we start to feel that wave of embarrassment come our way, we must remind ourselves that nobody else is sitting awake at night thinking about our mistakes. They're getting on with their lives. As the saying goes, it's none of your business what anyone else thinks of you.

We can take an extra step by showing people their mistakes are just that—mistakes. Remind them that it's okay. Reassure them that it's not a reflection of who they are, and you might help them build up their resilience. Being kind and connected to others is a surefire way to strengthen your own resilience and sense of empowerment.

If you are someone who struggles with shutting out possible comments and judgements from others, the best way to give yourself a break is to spend time with more accepting people. Choose an environment without people who make you feel you have anything to prove beyond what's required of you. The less time you spend feeling small, the more time you have to grow.

Having a non-supportive and highly judgmental group of individuals around you is going to damage your sense of self, hinder your deathless grieving process, cause more shame, and exacerbate the overblown implications effect. As such, it becomes more difficult to switch off the buzzing feeling that everyone around you is judging you. If you feel that this sounds like your group of friends, it might be time to walk away and find people who truly want to support your journey to empowerment.

I've spent a lot of time alone on my journey to empowerment. I've been surrounded by people who wanted to see me fail, and even though I stayed in those friendships I knew deep down they didn't want the best for me. But I was afraid to be alone. When I finally stepped away, I actually felt *less* lonely than I did with people around. My choice also allowed me to make space for new people in my life—ones that genuinely wanted the best for me.

Ms. Moon wanted what was best for me. My dad wants what's best for me. In my professional life, my mentors want what's best for me. I have cultivated a supportive environment for myself that doesn't rely on my successes, failures, or progress. These people love me for who I am, when I'm at my best and when I'm not. I'll spend some time showing proof of this in later chapters, but for now, know that the people I surround myself with play a large part in how I treat myself.

Chapter 7

Building Resilience Through Mindfulness

*"I count him braver who overcomes his desires
than him who conquers his enemies,
for the hardest victory is over self."*
–Aristotle

P lenty of people supported me on my journey to empowerment, but my progress was contingent on the work of one
specific person: me. It was my responsibility to sort through
my emotions and improve my coping mechanisms. It was up to
me to manage my self-concept and find growth opportunities. I'd
faced my shame, laid it all out in front of me, and that was a task in
itself…next, I had to find a way to move through it and finally let it
go. And to do that, I needed a stronger sense of resilience.

A strong resilience is the ultimate state of "I'm rubber, you're
glue." When you practice resilience, you practice bouncing back

after difficult moments. Resilience allows you to adapt to new situations by accepting their demands and moving through them. Resilience is shown in small ways, like letting a nasty comment bounce off of you. Sometimes, resilience is practiced in larger ways, like coping with change, loss, and uncertainty.

Showing resilience means recognizing your faults, adapting to your capabilities, and developing a positive outlook on your life. Mindfulness helps us accomplish these goals, but it's only one component of a bigger picture. If we are to truly assert control over our behaviors, we must know ourselves from the inside out. We must understand what's going on beneath our surface thoughts and how it affects our emotions, behaviors, and decisions.

For most of us, resilience isn't a trait that comes naturally. Humans build up resilience over time. We do this by getting to know our bodies and minds. Once we have a better understanding of the mechanics of shame and empowerment, we can use that information to train up resilience with mental exercises.

Yes, I'm talking about mindfulness—but this isn't your average self-help exploration of the concept. This chapter takes a deep dive into the science of mindful practices. Dozens of books cover how mindfulness improves mindset, and we're going to cover that, too, but we're also going to go further. We're going to examine *why* mindfulness makes a difference and *how* it improves the mental state.

What is mindfulness? Anyone who's laid down to sleep after a hard day knows how difficult it is to stop the mind from wandering. Sometimes it wanders into harmless thoughts, but other times it dredges up shameful memories, negative self-talk, and possible future stressors. Mindfulness is simply the act of redirecting the wandering mind back toward the present and focusing on what is, not what was or what could be.

Over the last two decades, studies into the benefits of mindfulness exploded. Scientists are exploring how mindfulness increases emotional awareness, improves trauma recovery, strengthens resilience, and improves cognitive control. The discoveries made are more revealing than scientists originally expected. Practicing mindfulness, it turns out, also has a number of physical health benefits such as alleviating symptoms of stress, reducing anxiety and depression, protecting against chronic pain, cancer, cardiovascular disease, and so much more.

Before mindfulness became a mainstream concept, it was often dismissed as "woo-woo" guru pseudoscience. Except the man considered to be the godfather of modern mindfulness was an MIT graduate.[19] Jon Kabat-Zinn knew the stigma surrounding his studies into mindfulness. He wanted to bring mindfulness to the public without diminishing it to "new age, modern mysticism, or just plain flakey." He had a steep hill to climb.

Kabat-Zinn started a mindfulness course for patients suffering from chronic pain. His goal was to host a mindfulness-based stress-reduction course to help people find peace in their pain. In 1979, Kabat-Zinn's course began at the University of Massachusetts Medical School.

The first students were victims of industrial accidents, cancer patients, paraplegics, and people with chronic back pain. Most of Kabat-Zinn's patients spent the majority of their lives trying to avoid, ignore, or suppress their pain. So, when he instructed them to focus on their pain directly, without judgment or recoil, they were skeptical.

He gave them some clarity, saying mindful meditation "results in apprehending the constantly changing nature of sensations, even unpleasant ones, and thus their impermanence." Kabat-Zinn didn't ask his patients to imagine a future without pain, nor did he remind them of a time when they didn't suffer. He didn't ask for their opinions, likes, or dislikes about their experiences. He simply led them through some breathing exercises, a little yoga, and asked them to stay mentally present with him throughout the sessions.

By urging his patients to pay attention to the ebbs and flows of their pain, he helped them better understand their bodies. After the eight weeks were up, many of Kabat-Zinn's patients reported they found ways to "be in a different relationship with pain." Some of them noticed their pain diminished.

Today, almost fifty years later, UMass still holds free, weekly online sessions to practice Mindfulness-Based Stress Reduction (MSBR) and Mindfulness-Based Cognitive Therapy (MBCT). The results speak for themselves: MBCT prevents relapse into depression as effectively as antidepressants. In a two-year trial focused on MBCT, only 44 percent of patients relapsed compared to the 47 percent who relapsed on pills. On average, people with depression who participate in MBCT see a 37 percent reduction in symptoms.

Other researchers set out to build on Kabat-Zinn's groundbreaking progress in mindfulness practices. In a Harvard Medical School publication, Dr. Britta Hölzel and a team of researchers set out to create a framework for the benefits of mindfulness.[20] When this proposal began, there were plenty of studies on the benefits of mindfulness, but none of them dove into *why* mindful meditation works. What happens in the brain when practicing mindfulness? What mechanisms are at work?

Dr. Hölzel and her team set out to combine the existing research on mindfulness and design a framework other scientists could use to study mindfulness in-depth. They posited that mindfulness meditation exerts its effects in four components:

1. Attention regulation
2. Body awareness
3. Emotional regulation
4. Change in perspective on the self

Following the proposal, Dr. Hölzel continued to expand on Kabat-Zinn's research by conducting a study of her own.[21] She led a longitudinal study in which sixteen participants who had never practiced meditation before enrolled in an eight-week MBSR program. The participants underwent magnetic resonance imaging (MRI) scans before and after the program. Her study's results provided evidence for her mindfulness meditation framework in each of the four components she and her team theorized the year before.

The combination of Hölzel's proposal and her longitudinal study provided evidence that mindfulness changes how the brain functions by causing neuroplastic changes to multiple brain regions. They believed these four components worked together to make those changes, which in turn enhanced self-regulation—a crucial part of resilience.

Attention Regulation

Attention regulation is the introductory course for mindfulness. The most common mindfulness meditations are all about attention regulation, and nothing more. Focused breathing exercises are about focusing on the way your breath moves in and out of your body. Mindful sitting exercises require you to focus your attention on your posture, your breathing, and very specifically *not* on anything else.

Focusing on nothing but your present experience is harder than it sounds. In fact, when most people give meditation a try, they struggle to keep an empty mind. It's normal for the mind to wander off when there's nothing to entertain it. When this happens, it's not a big deal—calmly bring your attention back to breathing and start again. Over time, you'll get better at focusing on nothing for an extended period of time.

This mindful attention to nothing, according to Dr. Hölzel, improves executive attention when we *do* need to focus on something. One part of the brain, the anterior cingulate cortex (ACC) is responsible for enabling executive attention. It detects the presence of conflicts emerging from incompatible streams of information. When there's a deadline to meet at work that requires lots of effort in a little time, a mind with weak executive attention is likely to spiral into a panic. But when a mind with a strong executive attention faces the same problem, the ACC kicks in to focus on completing the next task, diverting attention away from the stress of an approaching deadline.

By improving attention awareness, we improve cognitive control, which in turn strengthens our resilience. Strong cognitive control allows us to ignore the more painful, stressful, or complex responses we may have to our environments. Just as meditation encourages its participants to focus only on breathing, executive attention is the underlying mechanism responsible for how well we focus only on the task in front of us.

Attention regulation also helps us snap to attention faster and more accurately. Researchers discovered that after participants practiced MSBR, their "alerting" instincts—their ability to achieve and maintain vigilance and preparedness—improved significantly. Practicing meditation to regulate attention can make even the sneakiest threat appear plain as day. It won't be long before we're snatching flies out of the air and saying, "I've been expecting you," when someone walks into a room unannounced. If eight weeks of meditation can turn us all into James Bonds, what are we waiting for?

On a more serious note, attention regulation comes at the forefront of mindfulness meditation because it is the base from which the other three components build up. Attention awareness is the first step to building a whole-body awareness, an emotional awareness, and self-perception awareness. And once we're aware of what work must be done, we can make progress on it.

Body Awareness: Interoception

Before we can empower ourselves, we have to listen to ourselves. Mindfulness is the practice of focusing on the subconscious signals coursing through our body. Our bodies send constant communication signals, but most signals fly under our conscious radar. This is good, since conscious awareness of all our inner signals would overwhelm us and cripple our ability to function. However, we often take for granted the accuracy of our body's signals, and if we don't learn how to pick up faulty signals and correct them, then we're prone to our body's automatic responses to false alarms.

In Dr. Hölzel's study, many of her participants reported that attending to their body sensations gave them a stronger awareness of their bodily states. When they walked, they noticed the sensation of their hands moving at their sides. When they ate, they noticed how different foods affected their thoughts, sensations, and emotions. When they were emotional, they took note of how their bodies responded to their experience. They accomplished this by practicing mindfulness and paying attention to their six senses: sight, sound, touch, taste, smell…and interoception.

Interoception is the recognition of the physiological signals our bodies send to our brains. Receptors in our stomachs tell us when we're hungry. Receptors in our bladders tell us when we have to use the bathroom. Whether we're hot, cold, hungry, full, thirsty, nauseated, itchy, or ticklish, our bodies let us know. Interoception refers to how well we listen.

Interoception helps us understand ourselves better. The better we know ourselves, the better we can address our own wants, needs, and behaviors. If we are to have true resilience, we must recognize that our hardwired associations and unconscious processes are not meant to be suppressed, denied, or run from—they are tendencies that, once brought to conscious awareness, can be controlled.

When interoception is channeled through mindfulness meditation, it takes focus away from pain and stress and redirects it toward what's presently happening inside the body. When practicing meditative breathing, interoception is sensing the air pulled down through your nose, making its way into your diaphragm where it feels a little lighter, flowing back through your body, and leaving through your mouth again. It's recognizing the adrenaline rush of arousal or sensing pain shooting through your nerves. It's paying attention to the weakness in your limbs that accompanies fatigue after a long day. Interoception helps you understand what's happening inside your body, and mindfulness reminds you that none of it is permanent.

An influx of empirical research surrounding interoception has appeared in recent years, and many of the studies overlap with mindfulness and resilience building. Researchers across fields as diverse as neuroscience, behavioral science, clinical psychology, developmental psychology, and more. Their studies show that our sensitivity to interoceptive signals can determine how well we regulate our emotions.

One region of the brain, the insula, is commonly involved in interoception. The insula also plays a large role in our consciousness. When spurred to life through interoception, the insula supports self-reflection by prompting us to question why our bodily state changed. It also helps strengthen our self-concept by bringing us back to basics before we examine what information is causing an interoceptive response.

Many of us think that we don't have time to slow down and reflect or listen to ourselves. Sometimes we're afraid that if we do listen, we won't like what we hear. But avoiding what our bodies are trying to tell us does nothing to help us heal and grow. Choosing to listen is how we stay aware of their influence. As such, it is up to us to decide whether we are willing to make time to listen and learn from ourselves.

If you think you've already mastered interoception, or that you have a strong sense of what goes on in your own body, you're in good company. Many people believe they're more in tune with their body than they actually are. After all, how hard can it be to monitor your own breathing, or count how many times your heart beats in a minute? (Are you thinking about it now? How much has your breathing changed since reading the last two sentences? It's harder to tell than you'd think.)

In a 2015 study, researchers asked participants to measure their own heartbeat by counting the beats per minute.[22] Then, the researchers played recordings of a basic beat and asked participants whether the beat fell in line with their heartbeat. They also conducted a questionnaire to learn how often the participants noticed their own body signals. The results were all over the place—some participants were spot-on, while others showed poor signs of interoception in all three tests.

However, the researchers discovered a more distressing result from their study: many participants who reported low interoceptive awareness also suffered from depression. In contrast, participants who reported high interoception suffered from anxiety. How is it possible to end up on two ends of a spectrum, but suffer mental illness on either side? The researchers dug deeper, and they realized anxious participants may be more aware of their interoceptive signals, but they often interpret the signals incorrectly. A small change in heart rate caused those with anxiety to catastrophize their feelings and amplify their stress levels, while the participants with depression hardly noticed...or didn't care.

After a traumatic experience, or subsequent loss of self, individuals often have difficulty reconnecting their mental and physical states. Their hearts race, their eyes well up, and their heads pound, but they don't know why. They're freediving without any sign of a tether, and they're in danger of drowning in their own emotions. It can be distressing to experience a total physiological transformation without knowing where the changes come from.

Many clinicians, when treating patients with trauma, depression, anxiety, or some combination of the three, start with interoception. They use mindfulness practices to help patients connect with their bodies and listen to inner signals. As these patients build a strong connection with their inner and outer experiences, they get to know themselves. The more they get to know themselves, the more they trust themselves, and the better they feel about their lives.

Emotional Regulation

Emotions give our lives meaning. Without them, life would be gray and dull, lived through empty eyes in a world without meaning. Our emotions drive our behaviors, our relationships, our career choices. They touch every aspect of our lives. Emotions are also essential to survival. They let us know when to fear things that could hurt us, what brings us pleasure, and where to focus our energy.

If we allow our emotions to control us and not the other way around, we will perceive our lives through a warped perspective. Without a sense of self-awareness to keep us in check, we end up behaving outside of our best interest. Anger turns to rage. Sadness becomes depression. Jealousy grows into bitterness, suspicion, and anxiety. We must regain control before we spiral out.

Mindfulness helps us regulate our emotions by redirecting our attention to the root of the response. Once we determine their causes, we can better examine how our emotions affect our experiences. Mindfulness helps us remain aware of our emotions instead of allowing them to drive us without our conscious knowledge. This awareness involves not only recognizing the experience of emotions and the physiological changes that come with them—such as sweaty palms, increased heart rate, furrowed brows, and more—but also having clarity over which emotions we're actually feeling.

For example, anger is an emotion often felt as a symptom of another, more "sensitive" emotional response. Anger can be a mask for pain, embarrassment, or sadness. Being mindful of how a sensation may look like anger but is rooted in sadness is crucial for regulation. Anger prompts your fight response—the blood pumps up to your chest, your muscles tighten, and your amygdala sends signals to prepare for an attack. However, if you can recognize these sensations as a response to misplaced anger, you can cool yourself back down and appropriately address why you feel sadness, and why that sadness prompted anger.

When Dr. Hölzel studied the brain scans of her sixteen meditation bootcampers, she was impressed by how much their brains changed. She noticed increased activity in the posterior cingulate cortex, the temporo-parietal junction, and the cerebellum. Each of these regions of our brains are vital in cognitive processes like learning new concepts, retaining long and short-term memory, self-reflecting, practicing empathy, and more.

With results like these, it's not surprising that mindfulness was eventually linked to psychological wellbeing. Dr. Hölzel's work suggests that mindfulness practices help the human brain rewire, in a sense, so it can respond more accurately to stimuli. This is crucial for our pursuit of empowerment because most of our brain's responses to stimuli—including emotional stimuli—are subconscious and automatic.

Much of what we feel takes place without our conscious awareness. As we develop, we create associations between behaviors and consequences. The behavior of touching a hot stove becomes associated with burning pain. The behavior of cleaning our rooms becomes associated with happy parents. The behavior of eating gas station sushi becomes associated with twisting gut pain. These associations then help direct future behavior to be more conducive for survival and pleasure.

This process of learning associations is called classical conditioning. When we're exposed to a stimulus that causes either pain or pleasure, we create an association between the stimulus and our response. The association eventually leads us to anticipate pain or pleasure from certain stimuli. The next time our hand grazes a hot stove, we yank it away before we even feel the heat. The next time we enter a dirty room, we struggle to focus until the room is tidied up. And the next time we catch just a whiff of gas station sushi, we'll want to throw up.

Given that these associations are typically formed outside of our awareness, our bodies tend to respond to emotion-eliciting stimuli in unpredictable ways. In many cases, our bodies respond to stimuli before we even notice. Like when someone waves in your direction at an airport and you wave back before you even realize: *A) I don't know that person,* and *B) they're not waving at me, but someone behind me.*

When your body has a false-alarm automatic response, the result is usually a quick flush of embarrassment. You can usually laugh it off. However, sometimes your body's responses aren't conducive to strengthening your self-concept or resilience.

Let's say, for example, you're an animal lover. You believe every creature on Earth, from the smallest ant to the biggest blue whale, deserves to live a healthy, happy life. You pride yourself on this belief and try your best to act accordingly. However, one morning, you wake up to a strange tickling sensation on your cheek. You rub the area and pull back your hand to reveal a big, fuzzy spider crawling through your fingers. You act before you think, and you smash the spider on the wall behind you. *What have I done?* you think, and your creature-caring heart immediately swells up with shame.

It's not your fault for smooshing the spider. Spiders are scary, especially when they show up unannounced on your face. You reacted to a stimulus that your brain believed was a threat. When a threat appears, there's no time to process its philosophical presence or justify its existence in your space. For your brain, spider equals threat, which equals fear, which equals smoosh.

However, replace the harmless, curious spider with a distant relative who wants to give you a bear-hug the next time they see you. If you're like me, the bear-hug is an unwanted trigger. And through no fault of your own, a well-intentioned greeting might cause an automatic freeze response. What can we do about that?

Each of our relationships, experiences, and traumas condition us in some way, tying a sensory experience to an antecedent. Unraveling each of these associations from our long-term memory would be an impossible task, but through mindfulness, we can focus on the present and recognize an association's potentially unwanted influence. Conditioned responses to emotional stimuli do not go away unless we care for them. They will lay outside of consciousness, affecting our sensory worlds as long as we allow.

It's not just the experiences we collect throughout our lives that condition us. Remember, we didn't arrive in this world as a blank slate. We are a product of millions of years' worth of evolution, and with that comes millions of years' worth of ingrained conditioning, and face-loving spiders are not the only stimulus our brains have evolved to perceive as a threat. It takes a conscious effort on our part to learn how to temper these automatic responses to stimuli.

Remember the insula? The part of our brain involved in interoception? In a beautifully crafted study using functional magnetic resonance imaging (fMRI), researchers set out to determine how the insula activated during periods of self-reflection.[23] Participants' brains were scanned while they reflected on their own qualities, and again when they reflected on the qualities of an acquaintance.

The scans lit up when participants thought about their acquaintances—this was unsurprising, as the insula is also known to take part in empathic responses. However, researchers also saw what they hoped for: unique insular activity when participants engaged in self-reflection. This was proof that the insula is a crucial part of our emotional processing, especially in regards to our emotional experiences.

It makes sense when you think about it (especially because you're using your insula). The insula is a crucial component of interoception, and internal awareness of our own experiences is a prerequisite for empathic emotional responses. We can't accurately empathize with other people's emotions if we're not aware of our own. We can't offer advice for regulating emotions without knowing how to regulate our own.

Recognizing the severity of your emotions helps alleviate any feelings of shame about the pain you feel. Healthy coping is not about suppressing painful, confusing, or unwanted responses. Instead, you can recognize that they exist and work to release them. We can ask ourselves why we feel a certain emotion, acknowledge it as a part of our experience, and then let it go. This process changes the way we appraise future emotional responses before acting on them, which helps regulate our experiences with ease.

Change In Perspective on the Self

Our self-perspectives are collections of our memories that are filtered through our emotional experiences, thought patterns, and past actions. To change our perspectives, we must remove the filters and give mindful attention to who we are in the present. Jon Kabat-Zinn's original course on MSBR involved teaching his patients about the ever-changing nature of their sensations. Just as every person's sensations, emotions, and perceptions are always in flux, our perspective of ourselves is an ever-changing collection of shifting concepts.

Dr. Hölzel's MRI results revealed three parts of the brain with heavily increased gray matter concentration by the end of the meditation course: the temporo-parietal junction (TPJ), the hippocampus, and the posterior cingulate cortex (PCC). All three structures are well known to impact the experience of the self, which led her to surmise that the structural changes were associated with positive self-reflection following the meditation sessions.

"It is interesting to note," wrote Hölzel, "that these structures form a brain network that supports diverse forms of projecting the self onto another perspective, including remembering the past, thinking about the future, and conceiving the viewpoints of others."

The more our brains engage in healthy self-reflection, the more positively we perceive ourselves. We feel better about who we are, what choices we make, and how capable we are as we move through life. Our self-concept may not always be within reach, but mindful self-reflection reminds us that no part of us is fixed. Our self-concept will return, and if it doesn't come back right away, we're capable enough to find it again.

Maintaining a positive self-perception is crucial for building resilience. The way you think about yourself matters. If you don't believe you're someone who deserves to bounce back, you'll fall flat every time.

One of the best ways to improve self-perception is to be mindful about self-talk. The way we talk to ourselves matters. The way we talk *about* ourselves matters. Our inner voice is the one we hear all day, every day. It is the voice we value above all others, even if we don't consciously consider its importance. Our inner voice is the narrator for our lives, always helping us interpret the world around us. If the narrator of any story doesn't like its main character, how is anyone else supposed to root for them to succeed?

Our inner speech allows us to interpret our feelings and perceptions, regulate our cognitions, and give ourselves behavioral instructions. As such, our self-talk affects how our emotions and behaviors manifest. Self-talk can be helpful in motivating and promoting effortful, healthy behavior and emotional reactions, or it can limit us, leading us to ruminate on negative thoughts that damage our self-esteem.

One 2021 study explored how self-talk impacted people's ability to succeed. Researchers examined a team of athletes to determine whether their self-talk affected their mental and/or physical performance.[24]

This group of athletes each ran on a treadmill for an hour while the researchers monitored their maximal oxygen intake. Next, the athletes were split into two groups and sent to self-talk training sessions. One group created and wrote down positive self-talk statements, and the other group did the same, but with negative self-talk statements. Finally, all the athletes hopped back on their treadmills for another sixty minutes of running. They were cued with their self-talk statements, either positive or negative, at the 20-, 35-, and 50-minute marks. After the hour was up, the researchers took cardiorespiratory measurements and salivary cortisol samples.

The athletes who engaged in negative self-talk had increased salivary cortisol, meaning their bodies were experiencing increased stress responses. These participants also reported they felt more exhausted by the workout than the ones who engaged in positive self-talk. Their repeated negative sentiments discouraged them from performing as well. This may be common sense…but it does nothing to improve my mood on leg day.

Negative self-talk also alters hormonal response patterns. When we tell ourselves we can't accomplish a task, that we're not good enough, strong enough, or smart enough, we send our bodies into an increased stress state. We experience not only psychological self-doubt—we also weaken our cardiorespiratory function and increase our exertion.

Sticking with research surrounding athletic performance, other studies have explored how athletes in a slump can improve their performance by improving their self-talk strategy.[25] These studies coached participants to reduce negative self-talk, whether through cognitive restructuring or thought-stopping. When participants swapped out negative self-talk for positive, their performance increased.

Improving self-talk as a form of self-management is often referred to as self-instructional training. This training is applicable to more than competitive contexts. Given that our inner speech works to regulate how we see the world, as well as how we understand our emotions, self-instructional training helps us break the cycle of negative thought rumination and regulate behavioral performance.

The simple choice to engage in kinder, more motivational self-talk strengthens our capability to heal and grow. Motivational self-talk helps constant mental processes like the learning of new skills, coping with change, and strengthening self-esteem.[26] It also helps us manage more complex mental challenges like coping with learning disabilities, dealing with pain, reducing symptoms of anxiety disorders and depression, and decreasing the likelihood of imposter syndrome.

The best way to be mindful of your self-talk is, counterintuitively, to step outside of yourself. When you find yourself trapped in an internal dialogue full of hurtful, discouraging language, it can help to think about another person hearing those same words. Would you allow your inner voice to speak to someone else like that? Would you speak to your best friend, your partner, or a colleague like that? If a close friend told you their inner thoughts sounded like yours, would you advise them to listen?

If the answer to these questions is a resounding "no," it becomes easier to dismiss the negative self-talk in your mind. The golden rule growing up is to "treat others how you want to be treated." I'd like to add an addendum to that rule—treat yourself how you'd like others to treat you, especially when it comes to how you speak to yourself.

Self-talk is one small component of the larger inner dialogue we're constantly having. Our thoughts about ourselves, our emotional responses, and the world around us come together to form our mindset. People usually refer to mindsets in a positive vs. negative context: the glass is half-full or half-empty. This may be a portion of how people view the world, but mindset consists of more than general optimism or pessimism.

Your mindset affects every aspect of your life. It determines how likely you are to take risks, how you perceive your failures and successes, and how you consider your ability to grow. Your mindset can limit your capabilities or propel you forward in life.

Growth vs. Fixed Mindsets

There are two common mindsets for humans: the growth mindset or the fixed mindset. A growth mindset involves understanding that our intelligence and abilities are changeable and improvable, and that we hold the power to grow and become better versions of ourselves. On the other hand, the fixed mindset considers our intelligence and abilities as assigned, unchangeable, and constant.

Growth mindsets are often found in people with an internal locus of control. If you believe you have the power to change, adapt, and grow, you're more likely to see the world through a lens of opportunity instead of obstacles. Fixed mindsets coincide with people who believe they lack the capability to make any meaningful difference for themselves or others.

Countless studies have examined how mindset impacts motivation, academic performance, productivity, achievement, communication skills, and a host of other factors.[27,28,29,30] The findings are unsurprising: individuals who have a fixed mindset respond to failure with helplessness and withdrawal, typically prescribing their lack of success to an inability to do better. This paves the way for a cycle of low or fragile self-esteem, shame, and self-doubt to thrive, consequently feeding an even stronger sense of hopelessness.

In contrast, when individuals with a growth mindset encounter the same failures, they are less likely to react with feelings of helplessness. Instead, they focus on meaningful improvement and effortful change. The growth mindset helps support a cycle of high and healthy self-esteem, as well as motivation towards self-improvement.

Although exploration into different mindsets is still in the early stages, some studies suggest that individuals who adopt a growth mindset show stronger connections between areas of the brain critical for error-monitoring and behavioral adaptation. There is also evidence of stronger activity in regions of the brain responsible for learning new concepts and displaying emotional regulation (ventral and dorsal striatal connectivity with the dorsal anterior cingulate cortex).

This research into mindset-based brain functions shows how much of our wellbeing relies on our mindset. The evidence suggests that a growth mindset has the potential to encourage neural efficiency. This strengthens mental processes in charge of monitoring for mistakes, staying receptive to feedback, and engaging in appropriate behavioral responses. In other words, it strengthens our resilience.

Let's say you head into work one morning and learn your boss is conducting performance reviews. You're still new to the company, but you came in with industry experience, so you're not worried. When you head into your review, you're confident about your level of effort and productivity. However, as the review goes on, it takes a sharp turn into negative feedback.

By the time you're finished, you realize it was the worst review you've ever had. Your train of thought has two possible tracks now: you either handle this stress with a growth mindset or a fixed mindset. A fixed mindset blames your unchangeable intelligence, capability, and motivation. You question whether you have what it takes to make it at this company. For the next few weeks, your workflow turns into a work trickle, since you're too dejected to pay attention to any given task.

A growth mindset recognizes the blow to your self-esteem without letting it keep you down for long. You can use the feedback as a guide to improve your work. You can remind yourself: *it's not so bad that I'm struggling. I'm still learning how things work here. What I need to focus on now is why my boss' perception of my work differed from my own. How can I stop that from happening next time?*

No one succeeds at everything the first time they try it. There's always room for improvement. A growth mindset allows you to keep that in mind when you face risks, challenges, and failures.

A perfect example of this growth mindset in action came from an interview response given by Giannis Antetokounmpo, a professional basketball player for the Milwaukee Bucks. Giannis was asked by a reporter whether he considered the team's playoffs exit as a "failure."

After a deep breath, Giannis said, "Do you get a promotion every year? In your job? No, right? So, every year you work is a failure? Yes or no?"

The reporter did not answer, so Giannis continued.

"No. Every year you work, you work towards something, towards a goal—which is to get a promotion, to be able to take care of your family, provide a house for them, or take care of your parents. You work towards a goal—it's not a failure. It's steps to success. I don't want to make it personal. There's always steps to it. Michael Jordan played 15 years, won six championships. The other nine years were a failure? That's what you're telling me. I'm asking you a question, yes or no? Exactly. So why did you ask me that question? It's the wrong question."

Giannis continued, "There's no failure in sports. There're good days, bad days, some days you are able to be successful—some days you're not. Some days it's your turn, some days it's not your turn. That's what sports is about. You don't always win—so other people are going to win, simple as that. We're going to come back next year, try to be better, try to build good habits, try to play better."

Internalizing a growth mindset shields you from the worst negative consequences of life. No matter your age, gender, culture, or creed, your mindset helps you overcome failure, maladaptive life experiences, low socio-economic backgrounds, and support psychological wellbeing. A growth mindset is not about the attainment of things or a growing bank account, it is about the growth of the Self.

A growth mindset keeps you realistic when you set personal goals. Growth mindsets support self-knowledge, which is crucial for understanding your own capabilities and limitations. Understanding your own psychological barriers is equally vital. If you're in denial about your emotional regulation skills, you can't take the necessary steps to improve. That means you're no closer to overcoming your shame, because you can't practice healthy resilience.

It's easy to assume you must take on a full-steam ahead approach to maintain a growth mindset. This isn't true. When I'm stuck working hard to achieve an unrealistic goal, deciding not to do it is personal growth, too. Taking a step back from the unachievable, going on holiday, and coming back to reevaluate is a sign I'm practicing healthy boundaries with myself. I may still accomplish the goal later, but by adjusting the milestones, limitations, or deadlines for myself, I successfully manage my capabilities based on my self-concept.

Personal growth isn't all about moving the goal up as soon as you reach it. Taking time to appreciate your accomplishments is also a part of maintaining a healthy mindset. Being present in your success helps improve self-esteem. You are not a machine, and if you decide not to step back and engage in self-reflection every now and then, you're going to burn out.

A healthy mindset, supported by self-reflection, positive self-talk, emotional regulation, and interoception, is the key to reaching empowerment through resilience. With the support of our self-awareness, we can successfully switch from a fixed mindset that may be holding us back to a growth mindset.

Many individuals who believe they have a growth mindset are actually stuck in a fixed mindset. They engage in self-delusion to justify their lack of success to themselves. We are all guilty of this to some degree; we're all human, and sometimes we get so wrapped up in our emotional experience that we can't see the forest for the trees. The important thing is that we recognize when we've fallen into fixed thought processes, take a step back, and reevaluate.

It is empowering to take back control of our behaviors and act with purpose. It takes great resilience to pause, reassess, and realign our motivations with our sense of self. When we center ourselves through mindfulness practice—be it meditation, yoga, or a trainer-led course—we connect with our self-concept. We move beyond simply listening to our emotions and learn to flow with them. We stop only hearing the symphony and begin recognizing each instrument, each melody and its message. We don't just listen; we feel. Then, we gain the control to harness positive experiences and release negative ones.

As we learn more about ourselves, how we feel and why we feel that way, we can make more accurate judgements about our abilities. We can move away from a fixed and limiting mindset, to one that enables us to grow and improve. Although letting go of thought patterns that no longer serve you may be difficult, uncomfortable, or even painful, the process will open your eyes to all kinds of new opportunities, benefits, and positive perceptions about the world around you.

Chapter 8

Self-Empowerment: Resilience is Required

"Good character is not formed in a week or a month.
It is created little by little, day by day. Protracted and
patient effort is needed to develop good character."
–Heraclitus

It was a breezy afternoon in Amsterdam, somewhere between the sweltering heat of summer and the crisp chill of autumn. My friend and colleague, Joe Navarro, was giving a presentation and invited me to join him. I was in the early stages of my first consulting business, and I recognized this event for its networking potential. I happily agreed to join, both to garner new potential clients and to watch the master at work.

Joe Navarro was one of the youngest agents to join the FBI, and he spent twenty-five years in counterintelligence and counter-terrorism. He became an expert in nonverbal communications, and uses his knowledge to apply his expertise in business, leadership, and scientific industries around the world. He's written dozens of books, hundreds of articles, and he's given innumerable speeches on the insights he's garnered throughout his life.

Joe is a poised and passionate speaker. As a nonverbal communications expert, he's a pro at engaging the audience, making them feel comfortable and attentive. He leaves his body language open and inviting. He smiles and encourages those listening to him. The more I watched him onstage, the more excited I was at the thought of giving talks half as good as his.

During his presentation, Joe must have noticed me hanging on his every word, because he decided to give me a shot. Completely in character, he shed the spotlight off himself and motioned to my place at one of the front tables. He asked me to stand and introduced me to the audience. Then, he reached behind a nearby podium and pulled out a second microphone. He asked me a question about my work, offering me a moment to shine.

The question he asked was one he knew I could answer easily. Funnily enough, I don't even remember what he asked. What I do remember: I should have known the answer like I know the back of my hand.

But something happened to me. I suddenly felt hot. My back prickled with beads of sweat. My palms grew clammy. I could feel my cheeks turning red and my throat swelling up. The longer I stood there, the more eyes I felt drilling into me. *Say something,* I urged myself, but I could hardly squeak out a single word. The answer to Joe's question was trapped behind a thick wall of panic in my mind. All I could squeeze out of my throat was a half-answered, confused response.

I hustled back to my seat after that, handing back the microphone like it was a hot potato. He gracefully slid back into the center of the presentation, mercifully letting me slink back to the periphery. I hardly heard another word from him—I was too busy giving myself a mental lashing.

Why couldn't I think straight? I kept asking myself. *Why couldn't I access the information I know so well?* I knew the science behind my body's reaction, but the lessons I've learned didn't resonate with me when I experienced the science firsthand. It took me years to fully understand (and accept) that although I am an expert of human behavior, my knowledge doesn't make me immune to the behaviors I study. I'm human too, and that means sometimes, I'm going to freeze.

When humans are in a state of psychological anxiety, fear, worry, or panic, our brains and bodies join us in such a state. This affects our psychological, neural, and physical performance. In numerous neuropsychological research studies, researchers have induced anxiety in participants to study why the brain triggers the stress response.[31,32,33] The results show that when our brains detect a threat, evolutionary instincts kick in. Our brains believe we're going to fight someone or fly out of danger, and cortisol floods our systems. Important functions shut down as the brain prioritizes survival.

Since an impromptu public talk in front of several hundred strangers was still a little stressful for me, my brain decided it was time to either fight off everyone in the audience or make a mad dash out of sight. Never mind how impractical both options were—remember, our brains haven't figured out the nuances of the modern social structure yet. My brain couldn't consider how a clear-spoken, brief answer to a simple question would resolve my problem. There were no resources left in me to recall information or speak plainly, because my brain diverted all my energy to escaping the limelight.

When humans experience this stress response we choke up, unable to access any memory or information we need. It feels so close we can almost touch it, but it remains elusive. Anxiety also weakens the connections between the logical brain center, the prefrontal cortex (PFC), and the emotional center (the amygdala). Usually, when we deliver a well-thought-out argument, these two brain regions are in direct communication, with the prefrontal cortex taking the lead to ensure that what comes out of our mouths is a logical response. However, when the amygdala alerts the PFC of a potential threat, like a thousand pairs of eyes staring up at you during a public speech, the connection becomes weaker, and the amygdala takes charge.

This is bad news. With the amygdala in charge, we're unlikely to respond to the perceived threat in a rational or logical manner. Instead, we're more likely to engage in erratic behavior. Once the perceived threat is gone, the cortisol is reduced and our nervous systems start to calm down, allowing access to cognitive capacities once again. But the moments in between the panic and the come-down feel like they last a lifetime.

I knew all of this. I knew biologically why I couldn't access the information, why my face turned red, why my throat tightened up. I tried applying all my knowledge of psychology at that time to stop the onslaught of anxiety, but it didn't work. It didn't make me feel better to know the science of why I felt that way if I couldn't do anything to stop it.

After the presentation ended, I felt off for the rest of the day. I was ashamed, embarrassed, and furious at myself. I felt bad for letting Joe down. I felt bad for letting myself down. Joe gave me my first big chance at public speaking in front of potential clients, and I blew it.

I went to Joe during a break later that evening. He saw me approach and smiled wide at me. I couldn't return the gesture.

"I really embarrassed myself, didn't I?" I said, looking down at the floor. "Do you think everyone thought I was terrible?"

Joe looked up at me and gave me a wide smile.

"You know what you're doing out there. You were just nervous. You don't need to prove yourself to anyone. You're here to convey—not to convince."

I let that sink in for a moment. I got so caught up in proving to a sea of strangers that I knew what I was doing, my desire for validation stopped me from sharing my knowledge at all. I grew overwhelmed by the possibility of judgment.

I learned a valuable lesson from that disastrous moment: true empowerment does not require you to prove yourself to anyone, nor does it require you to ignore valuable feedback. Being empowered means accepting the potential for growth while forgiving the inevitable mistakes. Empowerment requires resilience to stay strong.

Resilience: Bouncy, Not Bulletproof

The idea of being resilient in the face of criticism is confusing. Many people think that to be truly empowered, you must be untouchable. You can't be phased by any comments anyone makes about you, whether they be positive or negative. You must be bulletproof. This isn't a realistic expectation, though. Humans aren't built to be bulletproof—not from harsh judgment or from actual bullets. Instead, we can strive for a more...bouncy outer shell. Not every bullet will leave us unscathed, but most of them bounce back out of our realm of consideration.

As a social species, humans rely on feedback from social relationships, which is why not every comment hurled our way is worth ignoring. We need occasional feedback from people we care about to help motivate us toward growth. If we don't know what we're doing wrong, we can't improve, and we can't always see our wrongdoings for ourselves. We can't ignore others' judgments completely, or we'll miss the chance to improve as people.

We humans are designed to collect feedback from others, but we're not so nuanced that we can choose which feedback to consider and which to dismiss. We value feedback from close friends and family, but we're not immune to feedback from everyone else, not even if the feedback is only perceived. Our desire to earn positive feedback—and our fear of negative feedback—is why public speaking can be so nerve wracking. Even if no one in the audience vocalizes a nasty comment, the possibility of that happening is enough to send some of us reeling.

When you set unrealistic standards for being bulletproof, you set yourself up for disappointment. Instead, by practicing resilience, you take into consideration how your mind and body are affected by feedback from others. Then, you reflect on the feedback you received and ask yourself: *Is the person giving me feedback someone who cares about and respects me? Is their intention to be helpful or hurtful? How much of what they say resonates with me?* If the feedback is worthwhile, you let it in. If not, the feedback gets bounced like an underaged teen at a night club.

Empowerment is not a goal you reach by ignoring what others think, say, or feel about you. Reaching empowerment comes from mitigating how feedback from others affects you. Your self-esteem and self-concept must be protected by a layer of resilience.

That layer of resilience is a layer of reality. Negativity is an inevitable part of life. No matter how you behave, who you spend time with, or how you live your life, there will always be someone who has a problem with your choices. Your mother might not like your sense of style. Your friends might not like your taste in music. Your boss might not like your politics (and you might not like theirs.) Resiliency comes from taking those opinions in stride and mitigating their effect on your self-concept. You like what you like, you hate what you hate. As long as you're comfortable with who you are, you're doing alright.

Most of us face threats to our self-concept as early as grade school. I remember a horrifying threat to my young self-concept that haunted me for years. It happened during my school's celebration of Leavers' Day, a British school spirit day where everyone dresses up like "nerds": thick-framed glasses, suspenders, and pocket protectors. I felt strangely confident on Leavers' Day, as I was growing accustomed to my curvier body and felt less at home in the outfit than I had in the past. It felt more like a costume of my old, nerdier self. But on one of these days, a classmate overheard me gushing about a friend's Leavers' Day outfit and made fun of my voice.

"Doesn't Abbie have the most annoying voice you've ever heard?" he snickered. "It's so nasally and disgusting. She makes me want to bring ear plugs to school!"

I blushed and stopped talking mid-sentence. From then on, I tried my best to drop my voice low when I spoke out loud in school. I was ashamed of my voice even though I had no control over how it sounded. Additionally, the classmate who commented on my voice was not someone I cared about. But I didn't have a strong self-awareness, so every comment made about me felt true.

I know today that the boy was nothing more than mean-spirited, but that doesn't make the memory less shameful. In fact, I still feel ashamed about the comment *and* how I tried to change myself to fit the mold some stranger set for me. I see how I deserved better.

Instead of dwelling on shame from decades ago, I use that feeling to inform present decisions. I am better about not letting other people's comments affect my self-concept. When my podcast episodes air, or when my YouTube appearances go live, I avoid reading the comments. That way, I'm not tempted to criticize myself based on Internet strangers. Maybe someday I'll be able to read them and laugh off the cruelest remarks, but for now I act within my own boundaries. I'm a work in progress.

As you become more mindful of who you are, you gain a better understanding of what feedback matters. When people attack you with false judgments, you can look in on yourself and know how little those words mean in relation to your self-concept. When you have that strength at your core, remarks won't affect you the way they did in the past. As you deal with your shame and grow your sense of resiliency, your inner strength will be easier to draw on.

Resilience requires us to engage in self-reflection during adversity. In the previous chapter, we covered how the insula blooms with neural activation when we self-reflect. Social neuroscientists have shown that individuals with high resilience experience different neural activation (the insula and anterior cingulate cortex) than those with low resilience when dealing with stress. Specifically, the ability to perform well during times of adversity is associated with activation in these neural patterns. When we practice resilience, we look upon who we are, what we stand for, and how capable we are. This self-reflection provides a layer of security from other people's comments and the threat of being overwhelmed.

Given the societal pressure to be "mentally tough" in the face of challenges, it's common to struggle coping with negative experiences that affect your self-esteem. These issues can lead to adverse mental health and emotional distress. As such, it's not uncommon to respond to failure with self-criticism and perceive it as evidence that you're simply not good enough—not for approval, not for peace, and not for success.

Taking negative feedback, harsh judgment, and possible failure to heart can trigger your stress response. You've probably experienced this before: someone makes a comment that feels "too far," and you feel your blood pressure spike—maybe it makes your "blood boil" or makes you "see red," and suddenly you want to either blow up or throw up. That comment becomes a threat your brain tries to defend against. Without resilience, you stay worked up long after the conversation is over and the offender is gone.

Sustaining a stress response for an extended period of time is unhealthy. When rude remarks stick with you for hours or days, your stress response spikes every time you think about it. You dwell on what you could have said back, or how the situation could have played out in your favor, until you feel a stronger sense of control over the outcome. However, ruminating on these thoughts can have detrimental effects on physical wellbeing and mental health, and even lead to reduced performance since most cognitive abilities slow down during the stress response.

Resilience is key for making it through negative consequences without letting them cause lasting damage. Bouncing back after falling down is the only way to keep moving forward. When shame knocks you down, you must brush yourself off before you get back up and try again. It's easy to be blinded by stress, uncertainty, and judgment from others. But by taking a second to pause, to be mindful, and to allow our brain regions to activate correctly, we show resilience.

If you want to achieve empowerment, you must take care of yourself. The steps to self-empowerment are not to stop caring about what happens to you or what everyone thinks of you. They involve practicing resilience in the face of negativity. Self-compassion and self-care practices based on your unique needs strengthens your sense of resilience, helping you grow into an empowered, understanding person.

Self-Care & Self-Compassion

There is one person whose judgment is unavoidable no matter how strong your sense of resilience, and that person is you. The way you talk to yourself, take care of yourself, and show yourself compassion is paramount to your self-concept. After all, if you're not willing to show yourself any kindness or consideration, how can you expect anyone else to do it? To reach true empowerment, you must take care of yourself as someone who deserves to be empowered.

Compassion is a social feeling that compels us to act to relieve the physical, mental, or emotional pain of others. Picking up a dropped item for a stranger, offering a kind word to someone who's hurting, and caring for a sick friend are all examples of compassion in action. It is a sensitivity to humanity's emotional experiences, and a desire to make life a little easier for someone else.

Consider some of the most trusted people in your life. Why do you trust them? Is it because they're kind to you? Because they're honest with you without being cruel? Do they show you patience when you struggle, or empathy when you're upset? Are they invested in your efforts to be a better version of yourself? Overall, if you answered "yes" to most of these questions, you're placing trust in compassionate people.

Self-compassion is about how you treat yourself—how gracious you are when you succeed, how reassuring you are when you fail, and how much patience you have for yourself in the meantime. If you struggle to trust yourself to make decisions or take risks, ask yourself the questions above, but turn them inward: why should you trust yourself if you don't show any self-compassion?

When you are stuck in a shame spiral, self-compassion is difficult to practice. Sometimes when you behave in ways that make you feel ashamed, you stop feeling like you deserve compassion, or you start feeling like you deserve to suffer. Shame can make you feel unworthy of any sort of sympathy…even from yourself. But this mindset only serves to hinder your healing—you must fight through it. You do this by showing yourself the same grace you would show a trusted friend.

It's good to take responsibility for negative behaviors, but you must manage your responsibility with some self-compassion. If you internalize your mistakes and punish yourself for making them, they will manifest as blows to your self-esteem. Remember: how you talk to yourself matters. How you talk *about* yourself matters. When you change your inner monologue to reflect more self-compassion, you're better situated for a growth mindset.

Showing yourself compassion is a form of self-care. Self-care refers to how you take care of yourself and how disciplined you are about engaging in healthy behaviors. These behaviors range from small daily hygiene tasks, like brushing your teeth, to larger, more daunting tasks, like sticking to your gym routine, eating healthy meals, and maintaining personal boundaries. (we'll cover this in more detail in Chapter 10.)

Since self-care and self-compassion involve being kind to yourself in the face of failure, there are times when these concepts cross over into self-enabling. Self-enabling occurs when the actions you take to mitigate struggles actually perpetuate maladaptive behaviors. Being kind to yourself does not mean justifying giving up when you have the means to keep going. If you are struggling to overcome a challenge, giving up because "it feels too hard" or because you "just can't do it" is not a healthy form of self-care: it's self-enabling.

Since the line between self-care and self-enabling can be blurry, these concepts tend to take on some negative connotations, especially in Western culture. Self-care is often seen as a lazy form of self-indulgence. Rewarding yourself for a job well done is absolutely a form of self-care, but it's not all bubble baths and bonbons. Self-care involves looking out for yourself, which means practicing discipline and holding yourself accountable. Self-care isn't always easy, but it is necessary to maintain a healthy life.

Some people also consider self-compassion as a sign of poor performance. This is especially common in private sector jobs. Many people believe showing yourself kindness, patience, or sensitivity is weak or lazy. Why go home and look after yourself when you could finish up that proposal a day early? Why step out for a break at lunch when you could eat at your desk? These beliefs perpetuate unhealthy work-life balances, then surprise everyone when they lead to burnout.

When self-care and self-compassion aren't considered necessary parts of your routine, you risk burning yourself out. Burnout comes from pushing yourself too hard and moves you away from empowerment. If you ignore your personal limits and capabilities, pushing yourself past the point of healthy productivity, you'll inevitably run out of energy. Then, instead of recognizing your exhaustion as a sign you've broken your own boundaries, (which we'll discuss more in Chapter 10) you'll be tempted to engage in negative self-talk, chastising yourself for hitting your perfectly reasonable limit.

In the modern working world, it's all too common for hard work, long hours, and burnout to be part of the job. When I entered the workforce after graduating, I felt like I was in constant competition with myself and everyone around me. I told myself I could be better, and I wanted to prove I could work the hardest. I never stopped to give my body or my mind a break. Even when I tried to switch off "work mode," I couldn't. I was miserable, I was unkind, and I was lonely, but I was laser-focused on the one route to success I could see—working harder.

The result of my efforts was a tangled mess of shame and self-doubt, sprinkled with confusion. Despite meeting every one of my goals, I wasn't happy. My self-confidence was lower than ever. Looking back, I see the problem: I lacked enough self-awareness to know when to stop. I deserved a break, *needed* a break, but I didn't want to stop because I didn't feel worthy of stopping yet. I eventually learned that I would never feel "worthy" of stopping. I would either stop of my own accord or I would stop by burning out.

Today, I show myself more compassion, and my work has never been better. I take breaks throughout the day. I haven't yet mastered that art of stopping work when evening comes around, but I do treat myself to an occasional Saturday spa day. My outlook has completely changed. I am prouder of the work I produce. Sure, I'm not churning out the same quantity, but the quality is much better. I begin my days refreshed and end them satisfied with what I accomplished. I still work hard, but not at the cost of my wellbeing.

The working world isn't the only place where self-compassion can improve performance: researchers have discovered how integral self-compassion can be in competitive sports. In 2019, PhD candidate Laura Ceccarelli and a team of researchers conducted a study to determine how self-compassion influenced athletes' emotional regulation.

Ceccarelli was the Sports Psychology Consultant for the women's soccer team at the University of Manitoba, where she conducted the study.[34] She gathered a sample size of ninety-one athletes who competed at either a university or national level in one or more sports, like track and field, tennis, soccer, basketball, hockey, and more.

Once she had her participants, Ceccarelli conducted two surveys: one measured the athletes' level of self-compassion, and the other measured their fear of self-compassion. The study's hypothesis was two-fold: first, Ceccarelli believed self-compassion promotes adaptive physical and mental responses to failure in sports. Second, she believed there was an inherent fear of self-compassion in competitive sports that held back some athletes from experiencing a better recovery from failure.

Previous studies have shown that when tested, many athletes are hesitant to adopt self-compassion for fear that doing so would contradict their mental toughness and motivate them to succeed less than their self-criticism.[35] Self-reports from athletes demonstrated they were afraid to adopt self-compassion because it might make them appear weak or complacent to their teammates. However, Ceccarelli wanted to promote self-compassion as a healthy alternative to self-criticism in sports that actually worked *better* to improve athletes' recovery from missing a pass, fumbling a play, or losing a game.

For the experiment itself, participants were hooked up to a multi-modal biofeedback system that monitored heart rate variability (HRV) and parasympathetic nervous system responses. Then, researchers prompted them with a memory of a past sports failure. The more the researchers asked the athletes questions about their past failure, the more their HRVs changed. Some athletes, who rated highly in self-compassion during the surveys, demonstrated a calmer reaction than those who ranked lower. Specifically, the athletes who showed self-compassion had less reactive HRVs, demonstrating an adaptive reaction to failure and stress.

In other words, the athletes who were kind to themselves after recalling a past failure were less stressed about it. The athletes didn't avoid stress completely, but their practice of self-compassion dampened the effects. Their parasympathetic nervous systems activated, relaxing their bodies and mitigating their stress response. This process brought the athletes back down to their baseline vitals faster, which in a competitive, fast-paced environment, allows them to get their heads back in the game quickly.

It's good to have goals. It's healthy to work hard to accomplish your goals. What isn't healthy is sacrificing who you are for what you can do. Even as you push toward your goals, you cannot neglect your mental wellbeing, nor can you be passive about taking care of yourself.

Self-compassion is highly adaptive, and it's heavily associated with strong physiological and psychological wellbeing. The misguided belief that practicing self-compassion will undermine motivation for growth or hinder achievements doesn't hold up to scientific scrutiny. Self-compassion motivates growth, assists in confronting and correcting mistakes, and increases productivity to reach goals. Empirical evidence shows self-compassionate people may cope better with daily stressors, instigating more positive and healthy coping behaviors than individuals who lack self-compassion.[36]

It took years for me to realize that sometimes, even the act of doing nothing can be the most productive activity. I know I'm not the only person who's felt the dreaded fear that if you stop being productive for even a second, then you're unproductive. The middle ground doesn't exist. Relaxing, recharging, and taking some time for your self-care is productive in a different way. It may not produce paperwork, but it does take care of some much-needed maintenance for the machine that is made up of your body and mind. Taking breaks doesn't make you a failure—it makes you a human being.

I have rarely shown self-compassion in my life. I've often pushed myself to my limits, then pushed myself further. I pushed myself at work and at the gym. I gave up on relationships, my social life, and time with my family. Any time I did spend out with friends or family wasn't enjoyable because I was too busy thinking about work. When I moved into my own house, I never even went into my garden, and I could count the number of times I watched TV or sat in my lounge chair. The second I stopped working even for an hour, I felt like I was lazy, like I wasn't doing enough. I felt like a failure.

It's good practice to step outside of your goals and to-do lists for a little self-reflection. Check in with yourself to regain perspective on how motivated you are to work, how desperately you need a shower, or how beneficial a nice walk outside could be. You may have the intellectual capacity to complete a task, but check in with your emotional capacity as well. Does taking care of this task help you take care of yourself, or will taking a break for some self-care make the task easier in the long run?

When I'm struggling to show myself compassion, I practice by considering a different perspective. Mainly, I ask myself what

I would advise my dad to do if he were in my shoes. Often, the answer is vastly different from the one I have for myself. If my dad told me he'd been at the computer for twelve hours, I'd tell him to get up and go for a walk. If he told me he was hurt by a comment one of my sisters made, I'd tell him to be honest with them and try to talk it out. If he told me he needed to vent, I'd make all the time in the world to help him work through his issue.

I hold no judgment over my dad. I have only love, patience, and unending support for him. By taking my situation out of my lens of self-criticism and popping it into a lens shaded with compassion, I'm able to make a more compassionate choice for myself. This practice may not be self-compassion by the strictest definition, but it's a step in the right direction.

Self-compassion looks different for everyone. If you're a caretaker, you can improve your self-compassion skills by thinking of yourself as someone in need of care. If you're a plant lover, you can practice self-compassion by tending to yourself as you would your favorite plant. Whatever makes you feel safe, comfortable, and allows you to trust yourself a little more every day is the right way to practice self-compassion.

For me, a compassionate life means working to my best ability while allowing myself to take time away from work when I need it. I give myself time away from my office and give undistracted love and attention to my two cats. Since my work is what motivates my growth mindset, I'll probably never see a perfect 50/50 split between my work life and personal life. Still, I monitor my priorities to ensure I feel balanced, and I adjust as needed.

I wholeheartedly love what I do. I love socializing within a work environment often more than I do outside of a work environment, so if I'm left to choose between going out for a drink with friends or going with those friends to a science exhibit, I'll choose the latter every time. That's okay for me—it may not be okay for you. For many people, the thought of making work a priority over a personal life is horrifying. That's okay too. We are all different, and there is no right way to find balance except for each individual to do what feels right.

The all-important self-reflection practice can help you determine what choices feel right to you. Using interoception, self-compassion, and some mindfulness exercises, you can check in with yourself and ask: *Am I avoiding tough tasks because I'm not motivated, or because I am burnt out? Is there anything I can do to make these choices more manageable?*

Mental Health UK put together a list of common signs to indicate that you might be heading towards burnout. These include:

- Feeling tired or drained most of the time
- Feeling helpless, overwhelmed, trapped and/or defeated
- Feeling detached/alone in the world
- Having a cynical/negative outlook
- Self-doubt
- Procrastinating and taking longer to finish tasks

When you start to recognize these signs in yourself, it may be time to slow it down. This is scary when you feel there is too much to be done to pause, but if you don't, the work you complete will be lower quality until you take a break. Your cognitive resources are finite. You are a finite resource. If you want to be effective and efficient in your work, you must fuel yourself with the right mindset, motivations, and self-compassion.

The more you take care of yourself, the more you'll see yourself as someone deserving of care. You can start small by holding yourself accountable to small, daily acts of self-care. The time you spend improving your mental and physical health will pay off with a sense of accomplishment, more energy, a larger attention span, and slowly but surely, the growing belief that you are worth it.

Self-Confidence & Self-Esteem

Practicing self-care and self-compassion is the perfect precursor to building self-confidence and self-esteem. By showing yourself kindness after failure and discipline during tough times, you prove yourself worthy of time, energy, and eventually, success. As your self-concept grows stronger, your resilience grows along with it. You slowly build yourself up into a confident, empowered person worthy of all kinds of life experiences.

There are people who seem to have an aura of confidence surrounding them in all situations. The same people who feel at ease giving a public speech look just as comfortable in one-on-one conversations, leading small groups, or trying a new hobby. How do they make every new experience appear effortless? How do they avoid the looming threat of shame when they step out of their comfort zone?

These people know the secret to confidence: it comes from how *you* feel about what you're doing, not how others feel about it. The only way to look truly confident is to *be* truly confident. When you feel comfortable in your own skin, you're comfortable in any new environment, because you're operating from a place of familiarity, self-assurance, and self-confidence.

When I first started public speaking, I constantly felt like I couldn't breathe. The walls seemed to close in on me the second I thought about stepping out on a stage. But with every new speech, I gained a little more confidence, and eventually my excitement outgrew my fear. That doesn't mean my fear no longer exists, but it no longer overwhelms me, because I have enough confidence in myself to shut down those pesky self-doubts.

When a confident person tries something new, they are more excited about the possibility of success than the fear of failure. For example, let's say you're going fishing for the first time ever. You may not be confident in your ability to work a fishing rod, but you're familiar with the throwing motion you'll use to cast the line. You've been out on a boat before and you're comfortable on the water. You trust your fishing buddies to help you learn the process. Moreover, you trust them not to judge you when you inevitably tangle yourself up in the line.

If your confidence is lacking, you may be more concerned about looking dumb in front of your friends. You're less likely to laugh off any mistakes, even if they're normal for first-time fishers to make. You may cast a line or two, but the excitement of snagging a fish is drowned out by the panic you feel about reeling it in, releasing the hook, and tossing the wriggly creature back in the water. Every time your friends catch one, you feel a twinge of jealousy followed by shame. The whole event is less fun when you feel ill-equipped to enjoy it. Next time your friends invite you out, you'll probably stay home instead.

There was a girl that I went to school with, Anna, who was always the loudest in the room. She dominated every conversation, she shared her entire life on social media, and she had everyone around her hanging on her every word. I used to look at her and think, *That's what confidence must be like. That must be what it feels like to love yourself.* I wanted to know that feeling. I watched the ways Anna made herself the center of attention, always pushing to be seen. She took up any opportunity to be front and center of pictures, videos, and conversations, watching and reflecting on herself with pride.

It was incomprehensible to me at that stage of my life to stand in front of others and not be filled with the dread of judgment. I couldn't fathom looking at an image or recording of myself and feeling anything other than dread and insecurity. I was desperate to know Anna's secret so I could use it myself.

This was the expectation I set for myself: that confidence was built by the approval of others, and I would never be good enough until I knew how to love myself so loudly that everyone could hear it. But as I grew older, and after I spent many years working through my shame and learning to respect my own comfort levels, I realized I'd been looking at a symptom of something other than self-confidence. I'd been watching Anna seek validation.

There are different types of high self-esteem, some healthy and some fragile. They may appear similar at first glance, but it doesn't take long to distinguish the healthy from the weak. Individuals with fragile self-esteem are caught up in how others feel about them. They're always looking for an opportunity to prove how valuable and worthy they are. These people may consider themselves valuable, but only for as long as the external validation lasts. As soon as others' eyes are diverted elsewhere, the confidence dries up.

Self-confidence goes hand in hand with self-esteem, which is defined as the subjective evaluation of your worth as a person. Having high self-esteem means you value yourself, while low self-esteem means you struggle to see your own worth. Having high self-esteem is crucial for building self-confidence. It's almost impossible to feel comfortable in a space if you don't believe you deserve to be there.

When we struggle to hold on to high self-esteem and self-confidence, we search for that validation in external places. We compare ourselves to people we think project the aura of confidence we want to achieve. No wonder our self-esteem suffers—we're not doing ourselves any favors when we hold ourselves to other people's standards.

I used to think high self-esteem was loud and unmissable. I believed it belonged only to the people who walked into a room and announced their presence, commanding the attention of everyone in attendance, who happily struck up a conversation with anyone without an ounce of self-consciousness. I modeled my concept of confidence based on whose presence was the loudest—and I quickly learned how wrong that belief was.

In my experience, the individuals with fragile self-esteem are the ones who project their confidence loudly, like Anna, always seeking opportunities to self-promote. They're convinced the world is a competition for a finite amount of self-esteem, and they want to make it clear they're winning. However, this self-aggrandizing is unhealthy. It can backfire on social relationships in an instant, because it is often a flimsy mask barely hiding their desperate desire for external approval.

When you feel the need to seek reassurance of your worth from others, it is a sign to engage in some self-reflection and ask why it feels important. What is it in you that needs this reassurance so much, and how can you give it to yourself instead of seeking it from others?

Self-esteem that relies on what other people think of you will always be fragile. Once you learn to put your own needs first, identify what is most important to you, and make choices in line with what you want, not what feels expected of you, your self-esteem will flourish.

Healthy high self-esteem is not dependent on appearance, material goods, or other measures of success. It comes from valuing and accepting yourself for who you are. It means accepting your imperfections not as flaws to rectify, but as evidence that like everyone else, you are imperfect, and that's fine.

Research has shown that individuals with healthy high self-esteem don't focus their energy on trying to outshine or outgrow others.[37] They don't associate their worthiness with their social standing. Instead, they are content being on an equal plane with others, as long as they are staying true to their morals, values, and self-care standards.

I think everybody has the urge to compare themselves to others, but we're better off the sooner we step away from that compulsion. We can try to match the aura of empowerment others give off, but in truth, empowerment doesn't look the same for everybody. For some it's large and loud and for others it's small and quiet. You might find it hard to believe, but true empowerment for you will look exactly like whatever suits you best.

Herein lies the secret to true empowerment: it comes from meeting yourself where you're at and guiding yourself toward growth, not from setting and striving for unrealistic standards. Empowerment comes from showing yourself the same compassion, empathy, and patience you show in close social relationships. It comes from understanding your body is a fine-tuned machine, and the responses it unleashes are designed to keep you alive. You are built to survive, but more importantly, you are built to learn, grow, and thrive.

You'd never maintain relationships if you expected others to be perfect, so it's not fair to hold yourself to that unrealistic standard. Life is not perfect. Your responses to imperfections are not going to be perfect, either. Your thoughts will leave you before you speak them. Your emotions will react for you before you think through them. You will slide in and out of your self-care routines. You will never achieve the perfect self-concept. You will always be a work in progress. But that potential for growth? The ever-present choice to be better, make improvements, and learn to be comfortable in your own skin?

That's empowering.

Chapter 9

Empowering Others Through Kindness

"For small creatures such as we,
the vastness is bearable only through love."
–Carl Sagan, *Contact*

When you feel empowered, you're more inclined to share that empowerment with others through acts of kindness. Kindness is like fresh air: you don't always think about its presence, but you notice when it's absent. One of the greatest perks of empowerment is that it's an infinite resource. Sharing empowerment with kindness doesn't stale the air for you, it simply makes everyone around you breathe a little easier.

I went through most of my life feeling suffocated from a lack of kindness. I rarely experienced kindness from others, and it was even more rare for me to show kindness to others. That's not to say I was unkind—I wasn't. But I was neutral.

I was brought up believing life is hard and bad things happen every day. No matter how many times you get knocked down, you brush it off and get back up. You want to stay down? Tough. Get up anyway. I also learned that dwelling on the past is a fruitless exercise that only succeeds in keeping you on the ground. You've got to get back to work, because no one else is going to work for you.

These lessons were the lenses through which I saw the rest of the world. I didn't expect kindness from others. I didn't think anyone expected kindness from me. I never shared my personal burdens with others because I didn't expect others to help me out. I didn't reach out to help others with their burdens, not because I didn't care, but because the thought didn't cross my mind.

I believed most people existed in one of two states: falling down or getting back up. Everyone has their own baggage, and they're responsible for lugging it around. No one wants to add to their own load by taking it from someone else.

Then my dad had a stroke, and my reality shattered.

I came home for Christmas during the first year of my PhD program and experienced one of the worst moments of my life.

I wish I could say my wound from that night has healed, but I would be lying. For me to sit here and write about the intricacies of what happened to my dad would take more strength than I currently possess. But that's okay, my healing is a work in progress. I know that one day, I'll be strong enough to talk about it at length.

What I will say is this: I watched the man I love with my entire heart and soul fight for his life. To see a father who has loved me to the bones look straight through me with eyes that are not his... that is a pain indescribable in every sense.

I didn't register what was happening before I reacted. Time seemed to slow down. I didn't hear myself scream, but apparently

I did, and it was loud enough that neighbors down the street heard me. Suddenly the house was full of people. I couldn't see them clearly—my vision blurred along with my hearing. Everything was muffled. I couldn't see my dad, or my sisters, or the paramedics when they arrived. Even as people brushed past me, I felt worlds away. My body shut down to keep me safe, but it also kept me from helping my dad. Even now, years on, I feel the haze encroaching.

My dad got the care he needed and recovered fairly well. Once I knew he was safe, I turned my attention inward. I struggled to recover. I was still reeling from the trauma of seeing my favorite person, my protector, appear helpless in the face of a health crisis. I was also ashamed of how quickly my body put me into shutdown mode, making me incapable of helping as much as I would've liked. In my adult life, I wanted to protect my dad the way he tried to protect me. But when the moment came to protect him, I froze instead.

Once again, I was filled with shame over a reaction I had that was outside my control. My coping skills, my resilience, and my sense of empowerment were put to the test. And once again, I faltered. I worked myself to the point of exhaustion to avoid returning to a home filled with nothing but space to think about my dad. Still, I grew distracted, and the work I performed was riddled with errors. I fell behind and missed deadlines. The shame pooled around me as I floated along, unwilling to fight the current.

In progress report meetings, I made excuses instead of sharing my struggles with my supervisors. I didn't want to burden anyone with my problems. I kept falling down and picking myself up again, but I didn't want to admit how each time was harder than the last. Each day, to and from university, I sat slumped in the back corner of the bus, crying silently until I reached my destination. Then I wiped my tears, forced myself up, and carried on as best I could. I felt alone, useless, and desperate for someone to reach out a hand. But no one knew I needed help, so no one offered it to me.

I may have been desperate for kindness, but when I looked around, I realized I'd surrounded myself with people like me—neutral people who didn't see kindness as a default response. They were wonderful coworkers, but they were not people I confided in. They were not people I could approach while vulnerable. The professional environment we'd built was the perfect place for productivity, but it wasn't equipped for social empathy. It was stifling, and I needed some fresh air.

Sometimes a small gesture of kindness is all it takes to break someone out of their shame cycle to get back on the path to empowerment. You might be familiar with a small act like this. For example, have you ever had someone offer you the smallest kindness—a gentle hand squeeze, a spare tissue, or even a soft smile—and unexplainably burst into tears? Even if you held back the urge, perhaps a kind act threatened to shatter the fragile facade of "fineness" you were barely maintaining. That's the power of human social connections.

As I searched for support, I realized it was my own fault I couldn't find it. I wasn't generous about showing others kindness, so they weren't generous with me. No one was being malicious or purposely withholding a kind word from me—the gesture simply didn't cross their minds. To others, Abbie wasn't associated with kindness, empathy, or compassion.

We never truly know what another person goes through. Even when others tell us about their struggles, we don't know the depth of their suffering. We don't feel their heartache the same. Every human being is living their own experience—they have struggles and hardships, passions that get them out of bed in the morning and pains that keep them up at night. The people who need a little kindness don't always show it. When we need kindness from others, we're not entitled to receive it. If we're hoping others will show us kindness when we need it most, we must be prepared to do the same.

I went from thinking about my own desire for kindness to thinking about how much others might need a kind gesture from me. I now make it my duty to be kind, compassionate, and empathetic with others without needing them to ask for it. Life can be cruel sometimes, and bad things do happen every day. But rather than pick yourself up every time you're knocked down, you can work with others to support those rises and falls.

There's an "I" in Resilience

Part of what makes empowerment so difficult to achieve is how much it requires us to ignore others' experiences. Humans aren't designed for shutting down other people's successes and failures. That's how we learn most new skills—by watching people who already know it. When they succeed, we learn by copying their method. When they fail, we learn to avoid repeating their actions.

True empowerment requires us to focus on ourselves: our own goals, our own progress, and our own self-concept. The more we compare ourselves to others, the more differences we find and the worse we feel. We only experience empowerment freely when we stop basing it on how empowered others are—or how empowered they appear to be.

Humans have a habit of ranking emotional experiences. Our language is entrenched in this tendency. As children, we're told to finish everything on our plates because there are starving people in other corners of the world. When we complain about a bad day, we qualify how bad it was by mentioning someone else had it worse. There's an innate competition around how much people struggle, except no one wants to be the winner. This zoomed-out perspective on human suffering leaves us feeling like we don't have a right to be upset, not when others might be worse off.

When we compare ourselves to other people, good or bad, our own experiences can feel minimized. We pit ourselves against people who are trying to survive, not participate in a crisis competition. Then, instead of showing them kindness during their struggle, we resent them for making us feel small.

Let's be clear—other people's experiences do not invalidate ours. We're all living different versions of humanity. We suffer regardless of other people's suffering. Our accomplishments are not dampened by others' failures. There is no real competition over who deserves to feel hurt or happy. We'll never live in someone else's shoes, but we will experience our own life events however we're individually equipped to handle them.

One recent addition to humanity's shared experience compels us to associate tangible value with our unique experiences: social media. We've always had a tendency to compare experiences, but over the last few decades, social media applies literal rankings to the experiences we choose to share with others. Posts with high engagement appear on more feeds, and the types of posts most commonly engaged with are the ones people replicate.

This creates a cycle of curation, where people only feel compelled to share the most positive or negative experiences in their lives. When negative posts about surprise illnesses, tragic losses, and money struggles appear, they only succeed in making us feel pity for the poster—if not a little bit of schadenfreude. *At least I'm not deal-*

ing with that problem. But when online presentations of experiences are filled with lavish vacations, big promotions, and new relationships, they make us feel inadequate. We worry we'll never achieve the standards required for the kind of happiness on our feeds.

A 2020 study set out to examine how social media standards affect wellbeing. In their work, a research team based in the United Kingdom looked at how the representation of men's bodies on Instagram affected young males' mental health.[38] The team conducted in-depth interviews with a sample of young adult males who all had different levels of engagement with Instagram posts centered around male fitness and physique. They hypothesized that the more these young men engaged with unrealistic body standards, the worse they'd feel about themselves.

Their findings, however, told a different story. The results showed an even mix between the negative and positive effects of engaging with Instagram content under the hashtag #fitfam (a community for tips on exercising, training, and staying in shape). It was expected that high engagement with fitness model's posts may lead to negative self-view, higher pressure to conform, and anxiety due to increased competition. The study did find this to be true, but for some other participants, the opposite was true. These individuals showed an increase in fitness motivation, self-confidence, happiness, fitness knowledge, and healthy eating habits.

The difference, the researchers discovered, was in how the young men interpreted the content: as competition or motivation. Those who viewed the social media models as competition felt as though they needed to chase an ideal image, and subsequently experienced negative psychological effects. Those who recognized the content as inspiration for their individual health journey showed healthier behavioral outcomes from observing the material.

This, too, brings us back to the locus of control. If you have an external locus of control, you may feel the deck is stacked against you. How are you supposed to attract a partner when there are so many better-looking people out there? This competition spurs shame, because you don't feel like you have a fair shot at success.

If you have an internal locus of control, you see the fitness content as motivation for positive change. The models posting online are celebrating their wins, and the people watching are sharing in that celebration, hoping to have one of their own in the future. You know the power to improve lies within yourself. You're not out to be the best of the best—you're looking to be the best version of yourself.

Kindness is easier when there is no competition involved. Resilience is only possible when you're not so busy watching other people fall that you forget to stand back up. Or you feel dejected watching other people stand up and decide to stay down. When you focus your energy on yourself, your own journey, you eliminate distractions that make it harder to grow. You improve your own sense of empowerment, and in turn, you have the space to empower others.

There's no "I" in Empowerment

Empowerment is rooted in kindness shown toward others. When you feel good about yourself and your place in the world, showing kindness to others is a natural side effect. When I think about the people who inspire me, who empower me, who motivate me when I feel like giving up, there is one thing they all have in common: kindness. They are kind to strangers, to each other, and to themselves.

Every day, there are people fighting their own battles and wading through their own darkness who still extend kindness whenever they can. They reach out a hand to those who need help and show others how to claim their own power. This is the true result of empowerment: a sense of self-contentment that is so powerful, it compels us to share it with others.

I used to think neutrality was the only way to show strength. Kindness seemed like a form of weakness to me, because I falsely believed it involved taking on other people's problems and receiving external validation for doing so. I now know kindness is not weakness, nor is it a selfish act disguised as a selfless one. Kindness allows us to practice compassion and resiliency without treating those traits as finite resources that we take away from ourselves.

Have you ever stepped out of your comfort zone with a new look? Maybe your haircut is slightly different than usual, or you're wearing a new outfit that deviates from your usual style. Adjustments to your image, even small ones, can feel like bright, flashing lights that announce, "Hey! I'm super uncomfortable!" But when someone compliments your new style, whether it's a stranger or your best friend, you suddenly light up. You feel lighter, warmer, and a little more comfortable. That small act of kindness transforms your discomfort into confidence. You're both grateful for the compliment and grateful for your decision to try something new.

Kindness is about how we make people feel about us, but it's also about how we make them feel about themselves. In western culture, where people are more inclined to keep to themselves than in other parts of the world, it's common to leave people to their own struggles. We don't want to intrude, and we don't want to seem nosy. But kindness involves stepping in and asking those people if they'd like some help. When someone drops their groceries in the parking lot, we show kindness by helping them load it all in the car. When a friend keeps showing up late to dinner, kindness involves setting frustration aside and asking, "It's not like you to be late, is everything okay?" instead of, "Why can't you ever make it on time?" When we show others kindness, we help them feel more comfortable and capable.

Kindness can be practiced in a myriad of ways. It's in the way we speak to a friend when they let us down, allowing them to share their side of the story before reacting. It's in our silence when we withhold the good news of a promotion because our friend is celebrating their own new job, and we want to keep the moment about them. Kindness can be holding out your hand to someone in need of a friend and letting them know you are there. It is also about recognizing when someone wants to be alone with their thoughts, giving them space and privacy to deal with their emotions on their own terms.

Showing kindness doesn't just make us feel good—it's also healthy for us. Being kind to others is how we improve social relationships. Accepting kindness from others helps improve our wellbeing and theirs. It may not seem like a kind gesture makes much of an impact, but I say again: kindness is like a breath of fresh air. Even the smallest act of kindness can help us breathe a little easier.

Benefits of Kindness

Kindness and empowerment go hand in hand—-they're both crucial parts of a healthy wellbeing. It makes perfect sense from an evolutionary perspective for kindness to make people feel more secure in their social group. In fact, recent scientific discoveries take this concept even further, claiming kindness may be the key to happiness.

The desire for happiness is universal. It feels good to be happy. Happiness helps us enjoy life. But happiness feels like a personal endeavor. It feels like the best way to obtain happiness is to focus on our own goals, but it turns out that may not be the case.

Chapter 2 included a study about altruistic punishment—the idea that individuals will punish social offenders even though the punishment is costly for them and yields no material gain. In a 2017 study, a team of researchers from the University of Oxford carried out a meta-analysis of existing studies on altruistic kindness, examining if people are willing to lend a hand to others even though there is nothing to be gained from the interaction.[39] Specifically, they wanted to determine whether acts of kindness improved the wellbeing of the actor. After conducting a review of previous studies on the impacts of kindness, they determined the results weren't clear enough, so they decided to conduct an experiment of their own.

In 2018, two researchers from the original study, Lee Rowland and Oliver Scott Curry, branched off and designed a test to determine whether performing different types of kindness activities had different effects on happiness.[40] They gathered participants and split them into two groups. One group carried out one act of kindness every day for seven days, and the other carried out at least one novel (new to them) act that was unrelated to showing kindness.

The participants kept records of their acts of kindness and self-reported their feelings of happiness before and after the act each day. The results showed that performing kindness activities increased happiness significantly more than the novel acts. The results also revealed that those who engaged in a greater number of kind acts showed the greatest increase in happiness.

Making an effort to carry out a kind act at least once a day can improve our wellbeing by helping us lead happier lives. We feel good about doing good, and we feel good about making others feel good. That's how simple it is.

Rowland and Scott Curry went one step further in their study by examining whether the effects of kindness on happiness depended on the type of relationship between the actor and the recipient. For example, did showing kindness to a friend make participants happier than showing kindness to a stranger, or vice versa? The power of kindness was inarguable no matter what conditions were changed—there was always an increase in happiness compared to the control group's novel acts. It didn't matter whether the actor had strong ties or weak ties to the person they showed kindness. The practice of kindness still increased their feelings of happiness.

But wait, there's more! Showing kindness isn't simply an act that increases positive feelings, it also decreases negative feelings. Engaging in acts of kindness can help reduce stress levels. In a meta-analysis published by The American College of Lifestyle Medicine, Dr. David Fryburg set out to examine a group of pre-existing studies to identify coping mechanisms for chronic stress, exercises for resilience, and ways to improve overall wellness.[41]

Stress reduction tactics are critical to improve quality of life. Stress can be a silent killer, causing and exacerbating mental and physical illnesses, such as depression, anxiety, and cardiovascular disease. Dr. Fryburg believed that because kindness creates positive social connections, those connections can reduce stress responses. He set out to prove that kindness and connection can disrupt a vicious cycle of stress and disease by building resilience and lessening the brain's reaction to stressors.

In laboratory-based studies, viewers watched short, uplifting films filled with acts of kindness, caring, and compassion.[42] These viewers reported significant increases in feelings of happiness. They also self-reported changed behaviors following their viewing, increasing generosity by donating either time or money to others.

In another study, Dr. Fryburg and a team of researchers sought to determine the effects of kindness media. Patients and staff were recruited from a pediatric office's waiting room.[43] These participants watched either commercial children's television or kindness media streamed onto a waiting room television. This kindness media included photos of park rangers bonding with animals, two children hugging happily, and athletes helping each other across a field. After eight minutes of kindness media, Dr. Fryburg asked the participants about their feelings. Most of them shared feeling happier, calmer, more grateful, and more generous than those who watched the children's media.

Kindness is as powerful as it is empowering. Even stress, the silent killer, the ever-present mosquito in our ears, can be swatted away by a small act of giving, receiving, or witnessing kindness. Evidently, our positive attitudes and behaviors are contagious. Being in the presence of kind people makes us happier, and in turn, makes us kinder to ourselves. The cycle of kindness carries on and makes everyone a little better for being part of it. Think how much of a difference we can make to the lives of those around us, even the ones we haven't met, simply by being kind.

If that's not empowering, I don't know what is.

In my professional life, kindness was not only transformative for how I interacted with others…it also saved me from a miserable career track. When I started my first role as a university lecturer, I was excited to be surrounded by inspiring academics. These people were driven by the same passion and love for their work that drove me. I thought that we would all get together and share stories of hope and excitement for all that laid ahead in the world of academia. I was wrong.

I spent my first few months on the job reaching out to colleagues and superiors in my department, inviting them to join me on research projects that I had spent months, sometimes years, crafting. To my excitement, my invitations were regularly accepted. This, to me, only proved how empowering I'd find the work in front of me. I was ready to reap the rewards of a kind, supportive, exciting environment.

But the reality of collaboration didn't quite meet my expectations. Instead of pep talks and brainstorming sessions, most of my meetings were actually vent sessions with colleagues who regularly expressed their desire to quit. They ranted about feelings of contempt towards the system of academia. They shot down anyone who expressed even the tiniest bit of enthusiasm for their work.

Still, I did my best to create kindness in an otherwise stuffy environment. I kept up with the people who agreed to join me in my research. In academia, co-authoring a research study means sharing equal responsibility and accountability for a project. However, without fail, each of my studies fell to the same fate: their only contributions came from me.

Sometimes, my colleagues promised to offer support, then never delivered. I carried the workload alone, despite the benefits each "co-author" would experience from my work. I wanted to stand up for myself, but I feared doing so would end my research altogether. So I carried on.

The unequal distribution of work spread to other parts of my job. Course development activities, which were supposed to be a team effort, were left to me. Voluntary projects with no one on the sign-up list landed on my desk overnight. The air in the offices felt stuffier without the smallest acts of kindness to keep me going. My enthusiasm drained.

Instead of appreciating or even recognizing my hard work, my colleagues took advantage of me. They took my kindness for granted and used it to advance their own careers. They saw me as someone to benefit from without making a contribution to the work. The job stayed like this for a few months, and my passion flickered like a flame at the end of a wick. My happiness was at risk.

Finally, after almost a year, I hit my limit. I decided I couldn't keep working in such a draining, suffocating environment. I needed peers who cared, who wanted to share their passion with others. I needed colleagues who contributed to our shared projects. I needed a little kindness and compassion.

The choice to leave my dream career wasn't one made easily. I'd spent my whole adult life building to this position. The job I secured was safe compared to the unpredictable battle with the job market. However, I took the time to self-reflect. I decided facing the unknown was a better choice than staying in a place where I was overworked, underappreciated, and subjected to negativity on a daily basis.

So, I started my search. Instead of running my resume through every job board online, I reached out to a network of people who showed me kindness in the past. I attended events and met with people who greeted me with kindness and openness. I was nervous about approaching people in the private sector, but time and time again they proved to be some of the kindest people I'd ever met.

One of my research studies as a lecturer involved working with an ex-FBI agent who specialized in counterintelligence and behavioral assessment, Joe Navarro. We'd struck up a bit of a rapport, and when he learned I was hunting for a career change he recommended me for a position at Social Engineering, LLC. That act of kindness led me down a more valuable, exciting, and promising path than I ever imagined finding. If not for this introduction, I would never have met Christopher Hadnagy, CEO at Social Engineering, LLC, who further inspired me to be a more compassionate and accepting person. These two have been integral parts of my journey through shame to empowerment.

When I first started this new path, I'd never felt so alive or empowered. I finally achieved a healthy relationship with my self-concept, a strong sense of resilience, and my shame was under control for the first time in my life. I was like a cat with a laser pointer—ready to snatch up every opportunity in front of me the moment I saw it. But before I could tear off after new goals, I had to learn how to responsibly handle all of this new power. I needed to find a balance between sharing my empowerment with others and keeping some of it for myself.

Chapter 10
True Empowerment:
Finding Balance

*"For a man to conquer himself
is the first and noblest of all victories."*
—Plato

I know I spent the whole last chapter stressing acts of kindness, so this next part may sound a little counterintuitive.

Too much of a good thing can backfire, whether it's eating too much ice cream after dinner or giving out too much kindness at the cost of your own wellbeing. Kindness is not weakness, but showing kindness to others without first ensuring you're operating within your own limits is unhealthy. Push past your own limits on sharing kindness or eating ice cream, and you're bound to give yourself a stomach ache.

To show kindness in a strong, healthy way, you must first set boundaries around your own capabilities and comfort levels. Once you do that, you can communicate those boundaries with the people in your life. Not only will this process improve your relationships with others—it will also improve your relationship with yourself.

Kindness is strength when it's offered within boundaries that ensure you're not overworking yourself or putting your own well-being at risk. It's kind to help your friend move to a new place, but it's not a good decision if you have a bad back. It's kind to offer to babysit, but if you know nothing about caring for babies then you're not doing anyone any favors. It's kind to help a colleague with a work project, but if your own workload isn't manageable then you're setting both of you up for failure.

When I was a lecturer, I tried to show kindness to my colleagues by taking on all of the work when they failed to do it. I thought I was being kind to myself by completing work I was passionate about, but in reality, I set myself up to fail by overloading myself with enough work for a whole team. It wasn't until I started working with Joe Navarro and Chris Hadnagy that I understood the importance of putting boundaries around my acts of kindness.

Joe taught me a valuable lesson: being kind does not mean being a pushover, and it does not mean being a "yes man." You can be kind while still valuing your time, prioritizing yourself, and learning when to limit other people's access to you. In fact, it's much harder to be kind to others if you're not kind to yourself first.

As Joe and I continued working together, I learned true collaboration. My contributions were valued and appreciated. When Joe introduced me to his network, I met individuals who found ways to support each other without sacrificing their work-life balance. These professionals were making waves in their industries while still saving time for their families, friends, and volunteer work.

Joe helped me to feel comfortable, confident, and capable when delivering my work. When Joe recommended I apply for Director of Education at Social Engineering, LLC, I trusted him. He introduced me to Chris Hadnagy, the founder and CEO, and we hit it off almost immediately. How could we not? We're both passionate about the work we do, the people we help, and the science behind who we are.

I believe Chris is the perfect example of someone who cares deeply for the people around him. When I accepted the Director of Education position, Chris dropped everything to help me move from the UK to Florida. He helped me sort out my paperwork, set up appointments for my visa, and advocated for me every step of the way. Chris has shown me more kindness and compassion than I ever thought possible, and he's never once asked anything in return.

Not everyone is lucky enough to meet people like Joe and Chris. It's rare to meet people who want nothing from you but to see you succeed. However, we have the ability to make it more common by *being* those people. How do we accomplish this? Well, ironically, it starts with a little bit of selfishness.

We all experience difficult periods of life that feel like we're treading water just to keep ourselves from drowning. During those moments, we don't have the strength to help others, because all our energy is going toward making it back to dry land. There is nothing wrong with that. In times like these, it's okay to admit that the simple act of rising from bed in the morning takes all the energy we've got. There is no reason to feel guilty when you don't have the capacity to do more than survive the day.

When we feel like this, the kindness of others is a blessing, but the kindness we extend to ourselves is essential. No one else is obligated to show you compassion. No one else is responsible for your wellbeing. You must take care of yourself before trying to take care of others.

If you've ever flown on an airplane, you're probably familiar with the safety message from flight attendants: "Be sure to secure your own oxygen mask before assisting others." Some people find this message to be selfish, but if you run out of air trying to help someone else, you're both more likely to suffocate.

This message, when taken out of the context of an airplane emergency, still holds true for everyday life. On the plane, the flight attendant sets the boundary for you by instructing you to secure your own safety first. Out in everyday life, there is no attendant to tell us when to focus on ourselves and when to focus on others. We have to decide for ourselves what is inside our boundaries and what is not. This is a tricky task, but it's necessary for us to stay empowered.

True empowerment comes from how well we balance our own value with the value of others. We must do our best to avoid actions that hurt others while still acting in our best interests. act We want to stay mindful of others' opinions of us without letting them control how we feel about ourselves. We want to help others in need, but we must ensure our mask is secured before we secure someone else's.

It isn't possible to please everyone all the time, so it's not worth trying to do so. When you feel empowered, your desire for approval from others is lessened, but it's not gone for good. Setting boundaries helps you stay resilient in those inevitable moments where your best intentions displease others.

In my life, I've been optimistic and pessimistic. I've been weak, strong, loud, quiet, manic, depressed, and everywhere in between. The only constant in all those times was that someone, somewhere didn't like me for it. It took me a long time to recognize that as unavoidable. It took reaching empowerment to decide not to spend my life trying to win over everyone else.

We can make changes to ourselves, we can strike out of the box, but realistically we cannot change everyone's perception of us. Doing so would mean striking out against millions of years of evolutionary traits inherited to keep us alive. This may seem disheartening, but it's less harsh when viewed through an empowering lens. If we can't change human nature no matter what we do, why put in effort to be someone we're not? If all efforts create the same results—some labeling and judgment from outliers—our energy is better spent just being who we want to be.

We want to consider other people's experiences, needs, and opinions without allowing them to penetrate our wellbeing. We can accomplish this by understanding, establishing, and maintaining personal boundaries. These are not walls designed to keep others out—they are fences that draw a line between what is our responsibility to handle and what involves us lending a hand out of kindness.

Defining Boundaries

Healthy boundaries are the key to maintaining strong, healthy relationships. Setting boundaries means defining what kind of behavior you tolerate in your relationships, whether they're with your family, friends, a partner, a boss, a coworker, or a stranger on the street.

Boundaries look different for every individual, and they are often influenced by a person's culture, personality, and social context. The boundaries you set for some people may look different than ones you set for others. Personal space, for example, is a boundary set based on an imagined threshold around your body, but the limits look different depending on the context. Your parents can (probably) invade more of your personal space than, say, the sweaty stranger on the bus. Your boundaries around personal space change based on who's approaching you, where you are, and how you grew up.

Setting boundaries often involves thinking about interactions with other people, but some boundaries allow you to limit the ways you interact with yourself. For example, I have a friend who struggles with her weight. Her self-perception of her body makes her feel unattractive, and therefore unworthy of attention from people she finds attractive. This is especially hard for her in the summer, when she wants to enjoy the beach but doesn't want to wear a bathing suit.

One year, on a beach trip, she was so worried about her body that she almost skipped the beach altogether. She realized that doing so would only make her feel worse, so she decided to trick herself. She went to a nearby Target, picked a random bathing suit in her size, and bought it without going to the dressing room. She put on the suit at the beach without looking in a mirror. Without any idea how she looked, she wasn't as focused on how others saw her. She felt more comfortable. Since then, any time she feels self-conscious about her body in a bathing suit, she pulls out that Target suit and refuses to check her appearance. She shows herself kindness by distancing herself from uncomfortable, self-conscious thoughts.

Defining clear boundaries around the kindness you show others helps you stay safe, healthy, and balanced. Unfortunately, people often mistake kindness for weakness, and your willingness to engage in acts of kindness gives them an opportunity to take advantage. People who will take their fill of your kindness without regard for how they empty you out. Sometimes they don't even realize they're doing it—which is why it's your responsibility to set limits.

Showing kindness does not mean you are required to tolerate people who mistreat you, take advantage of you, or expect you to keep the kindness flowing indefinitely. We all have limits to how much we can offer each other. Even if the person you're kind to treats you perfectly, you are still entitled to enforce your boundaries and take a step back. Put on your oxygen mask before helping others put on theirs.

Boundaries help us feel safe and secure by giving us personal control. We can't control how others receive our kindness, but we can control how far we extend it. As such, you must ensure you're protecting your own wellbeing and not allowing other people to break through your boundaries. As I frequently remind myself, try your best to be kind, always, but never allow anybody to push you beyond your limits.

Setting Healthy Boundaries

There's a difference between defining your boundaries based on internal and external comfort. Healthy boundaries are set based on internal comfort: they surround what makes you feel safe, secure, and capable. Unhealthy boundaries are based on external pressures, like pressure to perform at work, conform to poorly-defined social standards, or tolerate unacceptable behavior from others. Unhealthy boundaries don't work well because they extend too far beyond our own comfort levels. And if we're not comfortable, we're not making progress.

Setting healthy boundaries and avoiding unhealthy ones starts with self-awareness. Before you can determine your boundaries, you need to understand your own capabilities, competencies, and comfort levels. This can be daunting—it takes a great deal of self-knowledge to recognize your own limits and allowances.

One of the most common boundaries people struggle to set is the boundary between their work life and social life. It's often called a "work-life balance," but it's referring to the strength of the line drawn between your personal and professional lives. This line might appear in different places for different people. It may move up or down as their careers change and grow. What doesn't change is how important this line is for maintaining a healthy, balanced life.

For example, when we're eager to do a good job at work, impress our bosses, bag another client, or we're too excited about the project we're working on, we drop that boundary between work and home. We stay in the office past dinner and come in before breakfast. We bring home work activities and work on them late into the night. This may work for us in the short term, but we're eventually going to struggle to maintain a healthy home life if we allow work to leak in every day. We'll be tired, strained, and we'll burn out.

Personally, I work a great deal more than eight hours a day, and it's rare for me to only work five days a week. five days a week. But I still uphold the boundary I set for my personal capabilities. If my work leaks into the time I require to rest and recharge, I know it's my responsibility to communicate that to my colleagues. Adopting this mindset has allowed me to look at my work life in a healthier way and not feel guilty for doing things for myself outside of my work hours.

Once a work meeting shows up on your schedule, it's no question whether you'll attend—so why not set up meetings for your personal life, too? Scheduling out time to practice self-care, spend time with friends, or even call a loved one is a great way to set healthy boundaries around how you spend your time. It helps you maintain balanced quality time with your social relationships, which is key for your wellbeing. It also presents a visual opportunity for you to better understand how you spend your time on any given day. Are there too many work blocks on your schedule? What about unblocked time you know you'll spend doom-scrolling online?

Social media is another great example of an area in life to set boundaries around. Once you've practiced mindfulness, self-care, and self-compassion, you'll learn a better sense of your personal boundaries. You know whether scrolling through social media makes you feel better or worse about yourself. You can limit how much posts affect you by changing how you interact with them. These sites are designed to make attention into a competition, and if you struggle with competing, social media sets you up to feel inadequate.

There are ways to mitigate those feelings of inadequacy online. For example, Instagram has settings to shut off the visible like counts on your pictures and on the pictures in your feed. This removes the literal valuation of each photo, making it easier to step back and enjoy the content for what it is. Suddenly it doesn't matter how much Internet strangers like a photo—it's up to you to form an opinion. Most sites have functions like these to remove some of the sharper edges of their content, so explore those settings and see what works for you.

In your personal life, setting healthy boundaries around your relationships help keep them strong. Boundaries between friends, family, and romantic partners require trust and mutual respect. They remove ambiguity around shared values, goals, and expectations. They make it easier to make prosocial choices that improve relationships. The more you know about what makes your loved ones comfortable and uncomfortable, the better you can interact with them, and vice versa.

Setting healthy boundaries is how you put your sense of empowerment to work. It takes great strength, resilience, and self-assurance to hold up your boundaries even when it's not convenient to do so. But choosing where you draw the line is only the first step; once they're drawn, you must communicate them with the people around you.

Communicating Your Boundaries

Although humans are remarkably adept at many skills, mind reading unfortunately isn't one of them. Your boundaries may be visible to you, but no one else knows where they fall. People won't know your boundaries if you don't share them. If you feel someone in your life is at risk of pushing you over a boundary, or crossing one themselves, you must let them know.

Communicating your boundaries involves being assertive, open, and respectful. It is not the same as making demands—you're not telling others they can't do anything—-but it does involve laying out clear expectations for the behaviors you tolerate from others. If they choose to press forward, that's their choice, but they're making it knowing that it will have negative consequences for your relationship.

As an example, let's say you're spending time with a friend of yours. We'll call him Zeke. You love hanging out with Zeke, but you're not keen on Zeke's friend, Jimmy. Jimmy is disrespectful—he's always talking over you, insulting you, and calling you out for your niche interests. You've tried asking Jimmy politely to stop being so rude, but he either laughs it off or causes a scene. You've tried to explain to Jimmy how his comments hurt, but he doesn't listen. You've tried to avoid him, but you still want to hang out with Zeke, who doesn't mind Jimmy's comments (because they're not directed at him.) You decide to set a boundary around your interactions with Jimmy to save yourself from the frustration, embarrassment, and stress.

Communicating this boundary can be broken down into three steps (plus a bonus step):

1. **Explain your boundary clearly, calmly, and straight-forwardly.**

    In this case, you can pull Jimmy and Zeke aside next time you're together and define your boundary. Express that you're no longer interested in communicating with Jimmy beyond basic social pleasantries. You may share a friend, but you're not friends with each other.

    When you deliver your boundary, don't raise your voice or derail yourself with apologies or defenses. Stick to expressing your limits and dismiss any issues Jimmy has with them. After all, these boundaries aren't for Jimmy—he missed his chance to weigh in when he ignored your previous attempts to talk about the issue.

2. **State your needs by directly telling them what you want.**
    Here, you can tell Jimmy that you're comfortable with basic hellos and goodbyes, but you're not willing to engage in a conversation with him, since so many talks with him before have made you feel disrespected. You'll still go to parties with Zeke and see Jimmy around, but you're done hanging out as just the three of you. You'd like to stay friends with

Zeke and be cordial with Jimmy, and this boundary around communication is how you're willing to make that happen.

3. **Set consequences for crossing or violating a boundary.**
   Since you're not demanding anything from people, you must explain to them what will happen if they choose to ignore the boundary you set. Jimmy may continue to try striking up conversations with you. You don't have control over his actions, but you do have control over how you respond. Let Jimmy know that you will politely dismiss yourself from any conversation he starts. Or, if he continues to break the boundary, you'll stop attending any events with him and Zeke altogether, which will probably upset Zeke by asking him to choose between his friends.

4. **Accept any discomfort that follows.**
   Jimmy is unlikely to take your boundary in stride. He'll probably be unhappy. If he hasn't listened in the past, it's doubtful he'll listen now. He might feel disrespected here too, despite the irony. That's okay. You've done your part by communicating your boundary. Now it's time to uphold it.

This example isn't perfect—if it were, Zeke would intervene on his own and stop his friend from being rude to you. But the world isn't perfect and neither are the people in it. Maybe Zeke has his own strained relationship to work out with Jimmy. Maybe he's not familiar with boundaries and doesn't know how to help you. If hypothetical Zeke's actions upset you as well, you can use the same formula to set healthy boundaries around his friendship, too.

At first, communicating your boundaries with others may make you feel selfish, guilty, or uncomfortable. This is normal—some people grow up believing expressing personal needs is selfish or wrong. But if you choose to forgo your boundaries to avoid making yourself a little uncomfortable, you set yourself up for unhealthy relationships.

Holding to Your Boundaries

Part of the reason setting boundaries has a stigma around it is because boundaries are tough. They're tough to set, tough to communicate, and tough to maintain. It's difficult to be assertive with the people in our lives. Sometimes it feels impossible to be our own advocate. However, if you continue to move through your relationships without strong, healthy boundaries, your feelings toward others will slowly slide from resentment to burnout to a potential breakdown of your relationship.

You are worthy of respect. You are worthy of comfort, kindness, and compassion. But if you're not willing to show yourself these traits, it's hard to expect others to do so. You must first show self-respect by communicating that your boundaries are clear, will not be walked over, and are here to stay. And if other people decide not to honor your boundaries, you must follow through with consequences.

Many people end up shocked when boundaries are enforced, but it happens all the time. We may not use words like "boundary" and "limit" around the rules we set in our relationships, but they still exist. If I start dating a man and we decide to be exclusive, we've set a boundary around how we communicate with other potential partners. The consequence for violating that boundary is a breakup. That means that if he cheats on me, I uphold the boundary by dumping him.

The same concept applies to most relationships. The rules differ just as much as the people involved, meaning there isn't a clear set of standards from the beginning. Clear communication, honesty, and mutual trust is needed to establish those rules. Breaking those rules leads to a fight or the end of the relationship. It's the same concept as setting, communicating, and holding boundaries.

If you find yourself dealing with people who repeatedly break or push your boundaries, it might be time to reevaluate some of those relationships. Healthy relationships aren't built with people who manipulate, take advantage of kindness, or disrespect you. Ask yourself whether these people are worth keeping in your life: are they helping you maintain your empowerment, or are they taking energy from you that you need to support yourself? If limiting their access to you helps you stay healthy and balanced, it may be the best course of action for the time being.

Using Boundaries to Build Empowerment

Holding your boundaries ensures the words, choices, and behaviors of others aren't a detriment to our sense of empowerment. If we allow other people to affect us too much, we'll ruminate on the negativity, then fall into self-doubt and negative self-reflection, which leads to our self-concept suffering a nasty blow. We must find a balance between who and what we take to heart. Boundaries help even the scale so we can find that balance.

It's good to be kind, caring, and motivated to grow strong social relationships, but never at the expense of your own wellbeing or mental health. It's in our nature to desire friendships and to want other people to like us. It can feel like we need to prove we're worth their friendship or we're worth being liked. When we give into that mindset, we're more likely to compromise our boundaries for the sake of validation. We can easily end up devaluing ourselves, worrying too much about what people think, ultimately damaging our mental health.

You don't need the approval of others to be who you are, and once you stop looking for external validation, you'll feel freer. That doesn't mean you stop caring about others, or that you don't want close friends. It simply means you don't secure your self-worth from what other people think of you. You don't feel the need to prove yourself to anyone. You're there to convey who you are, not convince them you're worth knowing.

As Shakespeare said, "If we are true to ourselves, we cannot be false to anyone."

This is probably the most important lesson I've learned when it comes to resilience and empowerment: I don't need to prove myself to anyone. I don't need to hide old versions of myself from others. Today, I am Dr. Abbie, but I was once Party Girl Abbie, Drug Addict Abbie, and College Dropout Abbie. I've also been Lecturer Abbie, Big and Little Sister Abbie, Cat Mum Abbie, and a thousand more Abbies. I will be a thousand more before my time is up. I am who I am because of who I've been. I'll be even better in the future thanks to who I am today.

A little self-reflecting, finding my self-concept, and determining what my true values were above all else helped me change my behavior to better serve myself. Those choices also made me better at serving others. When I realized I could never convince everyone else I was right or that I deserved to be where I was, I discovered that the only person who needed to believe me was me. It sounds cheesy, but hey, it's the truth.

Figuring out who we are in this world is tough enough. We don't need to make it harder on ourselves by burying ourselves in shame, denial, or self-doubt. It takes tremendous strength and power to live in line with our self-concept. Life is better lived with a sense of resilience, self-compassion, and empowerment.

Every movement starts with one person. If every single person chose to engage in one act of kindness per day, every single person would be one step closer to empowerment. It isn't easy to maintain true empowerment, but it starts with being more accepting of yourself and others. It grows as you recognize yourself as a kind, compassionate person with plenty to offer the world. It blooms as you believe you are someone who is comfortable with their choices, past, present, and future. The decision to stop the shame cycle and move toward empowerment is powerful in itself.

No matter how long the journey takes, it starts with you choosing to move forward. The moment you take the first step, you become a work in progress, just like the rest of us.

About the Author

D r. Abbie Maroño is both a scientist and a practitioner in the field of human behavior. Dr. Abbie has been recognized by the US department of state as top 1% in her field.

Having completed her PhD in Psychology, Abbie became a Professor of Psychology by the age of 23. Abbie is now the Director of Education at Social-Engineer, LLC, and specializes in nonverbal communication, trust, and the psychological mechanisms underpinning human decision making.

Abbie is an active member of several internationally recognized research groups and was awarded reviewer of the year in 2020, from select journals, for her significant contribution to the academic community. Abbie is also an expert advisor, coach, author, and keynote speaker.

Endnotes

1   Page, Nanette, and Cheryl E Czuba. "Empowerment: What Is It?" Journal of Extension, October 1999. https://archives.joe. org/joe/1999october/comm1.php.

2   Fudala, Ayla. "The Good Life: A Discussion with Dr. Robert Waldinger." Lee Kum Sheung Center for Health and Happiness, March 10, 2023.

3   Smith, David V., Benjamin Y. Hayden, Trong-Kha Truong, Allen W. Song, Michael L. Platt, and Scott A. Huettel. "Distinct Value Signals in Anterior and Posterior Ventromedial Prefrontal Cortex." *The Journal of Neuroscience* 30, no. 7 (2010): 2490–95. https://doi.org/10.1523/jneurosci. 3319-09.2010.

4   Quervain, Dominique J.-F. de, Urs Fischbacher, Valerie Treyer, Melanie Schellhammer, Ulrich Schnyder, Alfred Buck, and Ernst Fehr. "The Neural Basis of Altruistic Punishment." *Science* 305, no. 5688 (2004): 1254–58. https://doi. org/10.1126/science.1100735.

5   Holt-Lunstad, Julianne, Timothy B. Smith, Mark Baker, Tyler Harris, and David Stephenson. "Loneliness and Social Isolation as Risk Factors for Mortality." *Perspectives on Psychological Science* 10, no. 2 (2015): 227–37. https://doi. org/10.1177/1745691614568352.

6   Peters, Brett J., Nickola C. Overall, Yuthika U. Girme, and Jeremy P. Jamieson. "Partners' Attachment Insecurity Predicts Greater Physiological Threat in Anticipation of Attachment-Relevant Interactions." *Journal of Social and Personal Relationships* 36, no. 2 (2017): 469–89. https://doi.org/10.1177/0265407517734655.

7   Kashdan, Todd B., Velma Barrios, John P. Forsyth, and Michael F. Steger. "Experiential Avoidance as a Generalized Psychological Vulnerability: Comparisons with Coping and Emotion Regulation Strategies." *Behaviour Research and Therapy* 44, no. 9 (2006): 1301–20. https://doi.org/10.1016/j.brat.2005.10.003.

8   Adams, Thomas G., Christal L. Badour, Joshua M. Cisler, and Matthew T. Feldner. "Contamination Aversion and Posttraumatic Stress Symptom Severity Following Sexual Trauma - Cognitive Therapy and Research." March 6, 2014. https://doi.org/10.1007/s10608-014-9609-9.

9   Fairbrother, Nichole, and S. Rachman. "Feelings of Mental Pollution Subsequent to Sexual Assault." *Behaviour Research and Therapy* 42, no. 2 (2004): 173–89. https://doi.org/10.1016/s0005-7967(03)00108-6.

10 Sagone, Elisabetta, and Maria Elvira Caroli. "Locus of Control and Academic Self-Efficacy in University Students: The Effects of Self-Concepts." *Procedia - Social and Behavioral Sciences* 114 (2014): 222–28. https://doi.org/10.1016/j.sbspro.2013.12.689.

11 Özen Kutanís, Rana, Muammer Mesci, and Zeynep Övdür. "The Effects of Locus of Control on Learning Performance: A Case of an Academic Organization." *Journal of Economic*

and Social Studies 1, no. 1 (2011): 113–36. https://doi.org/10.14706/jecoss11125.

12   Mali, Vishal. "A Study on Locus of Control and Its Impact on Employees' Performance." *International Journal of Science and Research* 2, no. 12 (December 2013).

13   Jaruwan Sakulku และ James Alexander. "The Imposter Phenomenon. International Journal of Behavioral Science. (2011):75. https://doi.org/10.14456/ijbs.2011.6.

14   Ramsey, Elizabeth, and Deana Brown. "Feeling like a Fraud: Helping Students Renegotiate Their Academic Identities." *College & Undergraduate Libraries* 25, no. 1 (2017): 86–90. https://doi.org/10.1080/10691316.2017.1364080.

15   Monfils, Marie-H., Kiriana K. Cowansage, and Joseph E. LeDoux. "Brain-Derived Neurotrophic Factor: Linking Fear Learning to Memory Consolidation." *Molecular Pharmacology* 72, no. 2 (2007): 235–37. https://doi.org/10.1124/mol.107.038232.

16   Hagenaars, Muriel A., Melly Oitzl, and Karin Roelofs. "Updating Freeze: Aligning Animal and Human Research." *Neuroscience &\ Biobehavioral Reviews* 47 (2014): 165–76. https://doi.org/10.1016/j.neubiorev.2014.07.021.

17   Galliano, Grace, Linda M. Noble, Linda A. Travis, and Carol Puechl. "Victim Reactions during Rape/Sexual Assault." *Journal of Interpersonal Violence* 8, no. 1 (1993): 109–14. https://doi.org/10.1177/088626093008001008.

18   D'Argembeau, Arnaud, Helena Cassol, Christophe Phillips, Evelyne Balteau, Eric Salmon, and Martial Van der Linden. "Brains Creating Stories of Selves: The Neural Basis of Autobiographical Reasoning." Social Cognitive and Affective

Neuroscience 9, no. 5 (2013): 646–52. https://doi.org/10.1093/scan/nst028.

19 Booth, Robert. "Master of Mindfulness, Jon Kabat-Zinn: 'People Are Losing Their Minds. That Is What We Need to Wake up To.'" The Guardian, October 22, 2017.

20 Hölzel, Britta K., Sara W. Lazar, Tim Gard, Zev Schuman-Olivier, David R. Vago, and Ulrich Ott. "How Does Mindfulness Meditation Work? Proposing Mechanisms of Action from a Conceptual and Neural Perspective." Perspectives on Psychological Science 6, no. 6 (2011): 537–59. https://doi.org/10.1177/1745691611419671.

21 Hölzel, Britta K., James Carmody, Mark Vangel, Christina Congleton, Sita M. Yerramsetti, Tim Gard, and Sara W. Lazar. "Mindfulness Practice Leads to Increases in Regional Brain Gray Matter Density." Psychiatry Research: Neuroimaging 191, no. 1 (2011): 36–43. https://doi.org/10.1016/j.pscychresns.2010.08.006.

22 Garfinkel, Sarah N., Anil K. Seth, Adam B. Barrett, Keisuke Suzuki, and Hugo D. Critchley. "Knowing Your Own Heart: Distinguishing Interoceptive Accuracy from Interoceptive Awareness." Biological Psychology 104 (2015): 65–74. https://doi.org/10.1016/j.biopsycho.2014.11.004.

23 Modinos, Gemma, Johan Ormel, and André Aleman. "Activation of Anterior Insula during Self-Reflection." PLoS ONE 4, no. 2 (2009). https://doi.org/10.1371/journal.pone.0004618.

24 Basset, Fabien A., Liam P. Kelly, Rodrigo Hohl, and Navin Kaushal. "Type of Self-talk Matters: Its Effects on Perceived Exertion, Cardiorespiratory, and Cortisol Responses during an Iso-metabolic Endurance Exercise." Psychophysiology 59, no. 3 (2021). https://doi.org/10.1111/psyp.13980.

25 Hardy, James, Kimberley Gammage, and Craig Hall. "A Descriptive Study of Athlete Self-Talk." *The Sport Psychologist* 15, no. 3 (2001): 306–18. https://doi.org/10.1123/tsp.15.3.306.

26 Shackell, Erin M., and Lionel G. Standing. "Mind Over Matter: Mental Training Increases Physical Strength." *North American Journal of Psychology* 9, no. 1 (March 2007): 189–200.

27 Rattan, Aneeta, Krishna Savani, Dolly Chugh, and Carol S. Dweck. "Leveraging Mindsets to Promote Academic Achievement." *Perspectives on Psychological Science* 10, no. 6 (2015): 721–26. https://doi.org/10.1177/1745691615599383.

28 Cooper, Julie B., Sun Lee, Elizabeth Jeter, and Courtney L. Bradley. "Psychometric Validation of a Growth Mindset and Team Communication Tool to Measure Self-Views of Growth Mindset and Team Communication Skills." *Journal of the American Pharmacists Association* 60, no. 6 (2020): 818–26. https://doi.org/10.1016/j.japh.2020.04.012.

29 Yeager, David S., Paul Hanselman, Gregory M. Walton, Jared S. Murray, Robert Crosnoe, Chandra Muller, Elizabeth Tipton, et al. "A National Experiment Reveals Where a Growth Mindset Improves Achievement." *Nature* 573, no. 7774 (2019): 364–69. https://doi.org/10.1038/s41586-019-1466-y.

30 Claro, Susana, David Paunesku, and Carol S. Dweck. "Growth Mindset Tempers the Effects of Poverty on Academic Achievement." *Proceedings of the National Academy of Sciences* 113, no. 31 (2016): 8664–68. https://doi.org/10.1073/pnas.1608207113.

31 Wingen, G A van, E Geuze, E Vermetten, and G Fernández. "Perceived Threat Predicts the Neural Sequelae of Combat

Stress." *Molecular Psychiatry* 16, no. 6 (2011): 664–71. https://doi.org/10.1038/mp.2010.132.

32 Harvey, Adrian, Avery B Nathens, Glen Bandiera, and Vicki R LeBlanc. "Threat and Challenge: Cognitive Appraisal and Stress Responses in Simulated Trauma Resuscitations." *Medical Education* 44, no. 6 (2010): 587–94. https://doi.org/10.1111/j.1365-2923.2010.03634.x.

33 Sherin, Jonathan E., and Charles B. Nemeroff. "Post-Traumatic Stress Disorder: The Neurobiological Impact of Psychological Trauma." *Dialogues in Clinical Neuroscience* 13, no. 3 (2011): 263–78. https://doi.org/10.31887/dcns.2011.13.2/jsherin.

34 Ceccarelli, Laura A., Ryan J. Giuliano, Cheryl M. Glazebrook, and Shaelyn M. Strachan. "Self-Compassion and Psycho-Physiological Recovery from Recalled Sport Failure." *Frontiers in Psychology* 10 (2019). https://doi.org/10.3389/fpsyg.2019.01564.

35 Sutherland, Lindsay M., Kent C. Kowalski, Leah J. Ferguson, Catherine M. Sabiston, Whitney A. Sedgwick, and Peter R.E. Crocker. "Narratives of Young Women Athletes' Experiences of Emotional Pain and Self-Compassion." *Qualitative Research in Sport, Exercise and Health* 6, no. 4 (2014): 499–516. https://doi.org/10.1080/2159676x.2014.888587.

36 Mey, Lara Kristin, Mario Wenzel, Karolina Morello, Zarah Rowland, Thomas Kubiak, and Oliver Tüscher. "Be Kind to Yourself: The Implications of Momentary Self-Compassion for Affective Dynamics and Well-Being in Daily Life." *Mindfulness* 14, no. 3 (2023): 622–36. https://doi.org/10.1007/s12671-022-02050-y.

37 Carlock, C. Jesse. *Enhancing Self-Esteem*, 2013. https://doi.org/10.4324/9780203768013.

38 Chatzopoulou, Elena, Raffaele Filieri, and Shannon Arzu
Dogruyol. "Instagram and Body Image: Motivation to Conform to the 'Instabod' and Consequences on Young Male
Wellbeing." *Journal of Consumer Affairs* 54, no. 4 (2020):
1270–97. https://doi.org/10.1111/joca.12329.

39 Curry, Oliver Scott, Lee A. Rowland, Caspar J. Van Lissa,
Sally Zlotowitz, John McAlaney, and Harvey Whitehouse.
"Happy to Help? A Systematic Review and Meta-Analysis of
the Effects of Performing Acts of Kindness on the Well-Being
of the Actor." *Journal of Experimental Social Psychology* 76
(2018): 320–29. https://doi.org/10.1016/j.jesp.2018.02.014.

40 Rowland, Lee, and Oliver Scott Curry. "A Range of Kindness
Activities Boost Happiness." The Journal of Social Psychology 159, no. 3 (2018): 340–43. https://doi.org/10.1080/00224
545.2018.1469461.

41 Fryburg, David A. "Kindness as a Stress Reduction–Health
Promotion Intervention: A Review of the Psychobiology of
Caring." *American Journal of Lifestyle Medicine* 16, no. 1
(2021): 89–100. https://doi.org/10.1177/1559827620988268.

42 Schnall, Simone, Jean Roper, and Daniel M.T. Fessler.
"Elevation Leads to Altruistic Behavior." *Psychological Science* 21, no. 3 (2010): 315–20. https://doi.
org/10.1177/0956797609359882.

43 Fryburg, David A., Steven D. Ureles, Jessica G. Myrick, Fran-
cesca Dillman Carpentier, and Mary Beth Oliver. "Kindness
Media Rapidly Inspires Viewers and Increases Happiness,
Calm, Gratitude, and Generosity in a Healthcare Setting."
Frontiers in Psychology 11 (2021). https://doi.org/10.3389/
fpsyg.2020.591942.

A free ebook edition is available with the purchase of this book.

To claim your free ebook edition:

1. Visit MorganJamesBOGO.com
2. Sign your name CLEARLY in the space
3. Complete the form and submit a photo of the entire copyright page
4. You or your friend can download the ebook to your preferred device

Morgan James
BOGO™

A **FREE** ebook edition is available for you
or a friend with the purchase of this print book.

CLEARLY SIGN YOUR NAME ABOVE

Instructions to claim your free ebook edition:
1. Visit MorganJamesBOGO.com
2. Sign your name CLEARLY in the space above
3. Complete the form and submit a photo
   of this entire page
4. You or your friend can download the ebook
   to your preferred device

Print & Digital Together Forever.

Snap a photo

Free ebook

Read anywhere